Dare To
BREAK THROUGH
THE IMPOSSIBLE
WITH CHRIST

SUZANNE PILLANS
D. Min. Th

New Wine Press

New Wine Press

Roper Penberthy Publishing Limited

19 Egerton Place

Weybridge

KT13 0PF

United Kingdom

All Scripture references are from the King James Version unless otherwise shown.

ISBN 978 1 910848 06 7

Cover design by Zaccmedia

Typeset by **documen**, www.documen.co.uk

Printed in the United Kingdom

Contents

Preface

This book has again been such a joy to write as the Lord has given me talks to give to others, to help set them free from sin, sickness and all manner of bondages, abuses and rejection.

The Lord then led me to put into a book these teachings, which I have also lived out myself through the years, in order to help others to get free as well.

Please feel free to use this book in your own home groups or Bible studies and share the teachings with your friends, so they too can find their freedom in Christ.

Every few months we also run special teaching, prayer and healing weekends at our Standlake Ranch near Oxford, England and you do not need to become a partner in order to attend.

We also have a weekly prayer and healing meeting every Tuesday 8-10 pm at Standlake Ranch.

If you would like to attend either the above, or receive quarterly newsletters please phone 01865 300099 or email or write to Standlake Ranch, Downs Road, Standlake, Oxfordshire, OX29 7UH.

Suzanne Pillans,
January 2015

Foreword

Another book in Suzanne's "DARE TO" series!

Did anyone dare you to do something when you were young, even though the consequences could have got you into trouble? But you still went ahead and did it!

But let's look at the word "dare" through the eyes of a believer in Christ.

Dare can mean, *"be courageous!"*

God said to Joshua these encouraging words,

> *"Be strong and of good courage, do not be afraid, nor be dismayed, for the Lord your God is with you wherever you go."*
>
> (Josh. 1:9 NKJ)

Dare can also mean, *"be bold!"*

> *"Now when they saw the boldness of Peter and John, and perceived that they were uneducated and untrained men, they marveled. And they realized that they had been with Jesus."*
>
> (Acts 4:12 NKJ)

The origins of the word "dare" can mean *"be challenged!"*

I sense that you have a deep desire to do "great exploits" for the Lord or you would not have picked up this book! Every book in Suzanne's "*Dare to*" series should "challenge us!"

Suzanne has put "pen to paper" and shared what the Holy Spirit has taught her and how we can all do the same.

Each one of us, as God's own special children, can ask ourselves, "What is holding us back?"

This book endeavours to show us that the victory of Christ's death, burial and resurrection has already dealt with it all! Everything that we will ever need (past, present or future) has already been paid for by Jesus. He took it all, He carried every burden, every problem. Suzanne explains that we can lay down "our crown of thorns" and replace it with a "Crown of Victory!"

Not many teach it! We all need to read it! But how blessed we will be when we learn to apply it to our everyday lives.

Sonia Stock
www.soniastock.org

Crown of Thorns to Crowns of Victory

"L-o-r-d," I cried out, "no one has told the students that they will not be receiving their bicycles this year! What do I tell them at their graduation tomorrow?"

I fell into a deep sleep. We were in Heaven, the students and many of the evangelists that we had trained were standing beside me. Suddenly angels came in from the left, each holding a golden crown on a tasseled cushion. The angels began to hand out the crowns to each evangelist. I was amazed at the crowns. Each one was different. The crowns were as if they had been intertwined with gold stitching. I also noticed that they were different sizes and were not given out as the world would expect, whereby those who had served the Lord the longest would get bigger crowns. But to some, who had not been serving the Lord as long as others received the bigger crowns! I was also given a crown.

Then all the evangelists looked at me. "Oh yes!" I thought "we need to walk to the Throne and place these crowns at the feet of Jesus."

I led the way down the misted aisle where multitudes of people faded into the far distance. We approached the Throne. This shone as pure gold and was about two meters high. I could not see anything above the throne because of the brilliance of the light, so I decided to look down at the floor instead which was also made of gold and you could see yourself in it as in a mirror.

The evangelists filed to both sides of me around the front of what looked like an oval and possibly a revolving throne. They all looked at me again for the signal to start to lower our crowns. We all, as one, began to slowly lower our crowns to the floor when suddenly a loud voice, that seemed to come from everywhere at once, said,

"These crowns represent your lives given for Me," and I woke up.

Next day I told the graduate evangelists about my dream. These one thousand and two hundred men stood up and with one voice shouted, *"Jesus is worth walking for! Jesus is worth walking for! Jesus is worth walking for!"* and they began to praise the Lord with all their hearts!

They were not interested in bicycles anymore. They had received something far better from the Lord Himself and the miles that they would have to walk for Him in the future were no less than another stitch of gold onto their future crowns in Heaven.

Jesus says in Matthew 6:19-21,

> *"Lay not up for yourselves treasures upon earth, where moth and rust doth corrupt, and where thieves break through and steal. But lay up for yourselves treasures in heaven, where neither moth nor rust doth corrupt, and where thieves do not break through nor steal. For where your treasure is, there will your heart be also."*

There is worldly treasure and there is heavenly treasure. There are worldly crowns and there are heavenly crowns. Worldly crowns are for this life and heavenly crowns are for eternity. We can decide now to take off any "negative crowns," the crowns that this world has to offer and replace them with the "positive crowns" that God has prepared for each one of us. The choice is ours!

In 1 Corinthians 9:24-25, Paul says,

> *"Know ye not that they which run in a race run all, but one receiveth the prize? So run, that ye may obtain. And every man that striveth for the mastery is temperate in all things. Now they [do it] to obtain a corruptible crown; but we an incorruptible."*

This is speaking of corruptible and incorruptible crowns. Worldly crowns are corruptible, heavenly crowns are incorruptible. The negative crowns that I speak of are sin, pride and being blinded by the deceitfulness of riches.

Isaiah 28:1 says,

> *"Woe to the crown of pride, to the drunkards of Ephraim, whose glorious beauty [is] a fading flower, which [are] on the head of the fat valleys of them that are overcome with wine!"*

But we can also lose our crowns.

In Lamentations 5:16 we read,:

> *"The crown is fallen [from] our head: woe unto us, that we have sinned!"*

The Apostle Paul says in 1 Corinthians 1:18-21,

> *"For the preaching of the cross is to them that perish foolishness; but unto us which are saved it is the power of God. For it is written, I will destroy the wisdom of the wise, and will bring to nothing the understanding of the prudent. Where [is] the wise? where [is] the scribe? where [is] the disputer of this world? Hath*

not God made foolish the wisdom of this world? For after that in the wisdom of God the world by wisdom knew not God, it pleased God by the foolishness of preaching to save them that believe."

The crowns of this world (of the proud or those trusting in worldly riches) can all be removed, through sickness or age, through theft or greed, or even through death. But far better crowns, far greater rewards are waiting for the believer. As I said earlier, oh that we may choose to put on those "positive crowns!"

The Lord's crowns are not handed to the proud, but to the humble! Not to the unrepentant, but to the repentant! Not to the unrighteous, but to the righteous! Not to those who trust in their own ways, but only to those who place all their trust in the Name of JESUS! The Lord took the *false* ways of *men* and replaced them with the *Crowns of Truth.*

In Mark 15:17, we read of Jesus on the cross,

"And they clothed him with purple, and plaited a crown of thorns, and put it about his [head]."

Little did those men know what they were doing, nor the meaning, nor the difference that Jesus came to make for man, to deliver man from sin, sickness and death and exchange these for His Forgiveness, His Healing and His Eternal Life.

The writer of Hebrews 2:9 says,

"But we see Jesus, who was made a little lower than the angels for the suffering of death, crowned with glory and honour; that He by the grace of God should taste death for every man."

Should not every man repent and turn to GOD? Put our trust in Him, the incorruptible? But this is our own free choice.

Paul says in Ephesians 2: 1-10,

"And you [hath he quickened], who were dead in trespasses and sins; Wherein in time past ye walked according to the course of this world, according to the prince of the power of the air, the spirit that now worketh in the children of disobedience: Among whom also we all had our conversation in times past in the lusts of our flesh, fulfilling the desires of the flesh and of the mind; and were by nature the children of wrath, even as others. But God, who is rich in mercy, for his great love wherewith he loved us, even when we were dead in sins, hath quickened us together with Christ, (by grace ye are saved;) And hath raised [us] up together, and made [us] sit together in heavenly [places] in Christ Jesus: That in the ages to come he might shew the exceeding riches of his grace in [his] kindness toward us through Christ Jesus. For by grace are ye saved through faith; and that not of yourselves: [it is] the gift of God: Not of works, lest any man should boast. For we are his workmanship, created in Christ Jesus unto good works, which God hath before ordained that we should walk in them."

He not only forgave our sins, but raised us up with Himself to sit together with Him in Heavenly places, so we are able to live a victorious life IN HIM.

Paul says in Colossians 3:1-4,

"If ye then be risen with Christ, seek those things which are above, where Christ sitteth on the right hand of God. Set your affection on things above, not on things on the earth. For ye are dead, and your life is hid with Christ in God. When Christ, [who is] our

*life, shall appear, then shall ye also appear with Him
in glory."*

Isn't that the most glorious promise?

Crowns spoken of in the Old Testament are spoken of
as "ornaments of dignity" as in royal diadems, crowns of
victory and conquerors' crowns!

Proverbs 4:9,

> *"She (wisdom) shall give to thine head an ornament
> of grace: a crown of glory shall she deliver to thee."*

Isaiah 62:3,

> *"Thou shalt also be a crown of glory in the hand of the
> Lord, and a royal diadem in the hand of thy God."*

Crowns can also speak prophetically of the victory of Christ
on the cross.

Isaiah 28:5,

> *"In that day shall the Lord of hosts be for a crown of
> glory, and for a diadem of beauty, unto the residue of
> his people."*

The verses go on to speak of those who sit in judgment,
things we see all around us in these last days.

This next verse, in Proverbs 16:31, also speaks of a
crown of righteousness that awaits us if we walk in His
righteousness, even in our old age.

Proverbs 16:31,

> *"The hoary head is a crown of glory, if it be found in
> the way of righteousness.*

Or the NIV says,

> *"Grey is the crown of splendour if it is attained by a*
> *righteous life."*

The New Testament is the fulfilment of the Old Testament, and brings the crowns to fulfilment right now in our daily lives; we can all achieve them.

Jesus bore a crown of thorns for us on the cross – thorns of sin, thorns of past hurts, sickness, and a multitude of problems. The Lord exchanged those thorns so that we should receive His crowns of victory because we choose to follow HIM.

In the New Testament we read about five crowns. The everlasting crown (also called the incorruptible crown) found in 1 Corinthians 9:25 is connected to the believer living a disciplined life. The crown of rejoicing (also known as the soul winner's crown) is in Philippians 4:1,

> *"Therefore, my brethren dearly beloved and longed*
> *for, my joy and crown, so stand fast in the Lord, my*
> *dearly beloved."*

Paul asks the Thessalonians,

> *"For what is our hope, or joy, or crown of rejoicing?*
> *Are not even ye in the presence of our Lord Jesus*
> *Christ at his coming?"*
>
> (1 Thessalonians 2:19)

Paul proclaims in 2 Timothy 4:8,

> *"Henceforth there is laid up for me a crown of*
> *righteousness, which the Lord, the righteous judge,*

shall give me at that day: and not to me only, but unto all them also that love his appearing."

The crown of glory (for godly leaders who are examples to the flock) comes in 1 Peter 5:2-4. The crown of life (also called the martyr's crown) is found in James 1:12 and Rev. 2:10.

The Greek word for crown is "stephanos," as in a laurel wreath that was placed on the head of an Olympic champion in New Testament times when he won. We, as believers, will be handed these crowns by the Lord on the Day of Judgment. They will signify some special act of service that we have done for the Kingdom of God, and how we have persevered through trials and lived our lives here on earth. (The rewards for those who *overcome* are slightly different from crowns.)

Every crown is precious, but let us look first at the crown of righteousness, 2 Timothy 4:8,

"Henceforth there is laid up for me a crown of righteousness, which the Lord, the righteous judge, shall give me at that day: and not to me only, but unto all them also that love his appearing."

Those in unrepentant sin cannot look forward to His appearing but will cower in shame, but if you live in righteousness, then you will 'love His appearing'! To those who seriously follow after righteousness regardless of difficulty or cost, the Lord will give the *gift of righteousness and His grace.*

Then there is the crown of rejoicing because the Lord is coming back for us,

"For what [is] our hope, or joy, or crown of rejoicing? [Are] not even ye in the presence of our Lord Jesus Christ at his coming?"

(1 Thessalonians 2:19)

1 Peter 5:4 describes the crown of glory,

*"And when the chief Shepherd shall appear, ye shall
receive a crown of glory that fadeth not away."*

Our evangelists were only interested in the soul winner's
crown. This was their crown of great worth. They were no
longer interested in receiving a bicycle, because their Jesus
was so worth walking for. Every effort in evangelism, every
sacrifice, every difficulty, every test, every trial, is nothing
less than another golden stitch in our victorious crowns.

The Lord has done it all. He forgives our sins and in
exchange gives us the gift of righteousness. He takes our
inadequacies and gives us the gift of the Holy Spirit. He
has also given us the authority of the NAME OF JESUS to
do His work. He even gives us of His own love. We can,
therefore, do no other than return the glory to Him and lay
our crowns at the feet of Jesus, our lives given for Him in
submission, obedience and love.

And Jesus responds with an even greater crown, the
crown of life, James 1:12,

*"Blessed [is] the man that endureth temptation: for
when he is tried, he shall receive the crown of life,
which the Lord hath promised to them that love him."*

"What about these last days now?" you may ask? Do we
fear what is coming on the earth? Even this question
is answered.

The crown of life, Revelation 2:10, 11,

*"Fear none of those things which thou shalt
suffer: behold, the devil shall cast [some] of you
into prison, that ye may be tried; and ye shall have*

*tribulation ten days: be thou faithful unto death,
and I will give thee a crown of life. He that hath
an ear, let him hear what the Spirit saith unto the
churches; He that overcometh shall not be hurt of
the second death."*

What more can the Lord do for us? He has done it all! He
bore the crown of thorns and now wears a crown of pure
gold, as prophesied in Psalm 21:3,

*"For thou preventest (goes ahead of) him with the
blessings of goodness: thou settest a crown of pure
gold on his head."*

We may have to suffer for Christ, which can also be likened
to our crown of thorns, but praise be to Him, who will
Himself exchange our crown of thorns and replace it with
incorruptible crowns, positive crowns! All we can do is
thank Him and praise His Holy name!

I am speaking to every believer, when I say, we have
choices to make.

We have a choice by the way we choose to live our lives
here on this earth.

We have a choice to lay down the crown of thorns and
put on the crown of victory. All because of what Jesus
has already done for us on the Cross of Calvary.

We have a choice to be average or outstanding if we
walk with God.

Psalm 34:14,

*"Depart from evil, and do good; seek peace, and
pursue it."*

2 Timothy 2:22,

> *"Flee also youthful lusts: but follow righteousness, faith, charity, peace, with them that call on the Lord out of a pure heart."*

1 Timothy 6:11,

> *"But thou, O man of God, flee these things; and follow after righteousness, godliness, faith, love, patience, meekness."*

As I said earlier, we can decide now to take off those "negative crowns," the crowns that this world has to offer and replace them with "positive crowns" that God has prepared for each one of us. We can ask the Lord to help us by His grace to do this.

For discussion

1. What is the difference between worldly crowns and Heavenly crowns?
2. What crowns should you exchange in your own life?
3. What will be the result of taking off any negative crown and replacing it with a positive crown?
4. Have you thought of responding with a prayer?

> *Lord, I come to you now.*
> *I take off this negative crown in my life and give it to you. (Name it)*
> *Please help me to walk in the positive crown you want to give me. (Name it)*
> *I place it on my head to walk in it now in Jesus' name.*
> *Thank you, Lord. Amen.*

Breaking Through the Impossible with Christ

Paul says in Ephesians 3:14-20,

> *"For this cause I bow my knees unto the Father of our Lord Jesus Christ, Of whom the whole family in heaven and earth is named, That He would grant you, according to the riches of His glory, to be strengthened with might by His Spirit in the inner man; That Christ may dwell in your hearts by faith; that ye, being rooted and grounded in love, may be able to comprehend with all saints what [is] the breadth, and length, and depth, and height; And to know the love of Christ, which passeth knowledge, that ye might be filled with all the fullness of God. Now unto him that is able to do exceeding abundantly above all that we ask or think, according to the power that worketh in us."*

Paul prayed this prayer for us, you and me, to live in the knowledge and revelation of it daily. Why? Because, Jesus is alive and makes it possible! It's not what *we can do* for God

18

that is important, but what God can achieve *through us*. It is how available we are that is important. The key to this is giving our time in prayer and waiting on God.

Prayer is practical. It is not just saying prayers, it is relationship, discussing issues, seeking His guidance and the Lord will answer. His answers are sometimes simple and sometimes profound, sometimes practical and sometimes impossible! We need to obey Him. Obey Him in the simple, obey Him in the profound! Obey Him in the practical, obey Him in the impossible! As we obey God regardless, He will confirm what He has told us to do with His 'signs and wonders following.' (Mark 16:20 says, *And they went forth, and preached everywhere, the Lord working with them, and confirming the word with signs following.*)

I have seen this to be so real in my own life. Not just once but many times. For instance two years ago the Lord impressed upon me that He wanted to use me to usher in a revival in Sierra Leone without even going there. "Lord," I said, "that is totally impossible."

"I will show you, my child, in steps," came the reply.

The following week I had an email from Freetown in Sierra Leone asking me if they could open up one of our Bible Schools of Evangelism in their town and I said 'yes!'

Next step, I was asked if I would give a sample lesson to the students by phone from England. I spoke on the "armour of God." They loved the lesson and asked me, "If we arrange for you to give this message via local radio, will you do it?" I said "yes" and did so.

Next step. There happened to be a Chief who lived in a town about four hours from Freetown who loved the message so much that he phoned the radio manager to request that I do a crusade over the telephone in his town!

The manager then contacted Pastor Bobor who arranged the radio programme with him and Pastor Bobor phoned me. I had never done a phone crusade before, but because the Lord had told me what He wanted to do through me, I said "yes" and sent Bobor some bus fare money to travel to the town. The crusade was a glorious success because the Lord showed Himself in power both nights and hundreds received Him as Lord and many were instantly healed. On the second night the Holy Spirit came in like a wind from the back of the crusade causing hundreds to fall on their faces in repentance. Pastor Bobor shared with me that the Chief was sitting in the front and said with tears, *"Today my town has turned from poverty to Jesus."*

Next step. As the weekly radio broadcasts continued 6 am every Sunday morning, an Anglican vicar phoned in to invite me to do a crusade in his town. It was arranged but got rained out all three days of the meetings. "Lord," I inquired. "This is not working." "Wait" was the reply. About half an hour later Pastor Bobor rang me and says, *"The people were so disappointed that the crusade was cancelled due to rain, that the vicar has arranged that you still give this last night of the crusade over local radio so the people can hear the Gospel Message in their own homes."*

This was my first radio crusade. I gave the Gospel message, prayed them through the sinner's prayer, prayed for the sick and handed back to the radio presenter who invited those who were healed to come and testify the next day at an Anglican church in his town. 175 people turned up to testify that the Lord had healed them.

Next step. I get a phone call at 9.30 pm on a Friday night from another radio station in Sierra Leone, asking me to speak on "How to choose the right President" because elections were coming up. Here I am on live radio!

"L-o-r-d," I whisper, grabbing my Bible and opening it anywhere, and my eyes are drawn to Proverbs 29:2,

"When the righteous rule, the people rejoice, but when the wicked beareth rule the people mourn."

I continued, ... "This means that the Lord wants a President who will rule Sierra Leone in truth, righteousness and justice. Why? Because sin, sickness and death have entered our world and our biggest challenge is to try and overcome it."

I then explained how sin, sickness and death entered our world through Adam and Eve eating of the fruit of good and evil, giving this world over to Satan in exchange for the knowledge of good and evil. This allowed sin, sickness and death to enter into the world. Then I explained what God did about it by sending His only Son Jesus to pay the price for our sin on the cross. I prayed the people through the sinner's prayer and told them to put their hands on their sickness or pain and say, "Lord Jesus, lay your hand on my hand and I will be healed in Jesus' Name."

I then handed back to the radio presenter who said, "We will now open the lines for those who would like to ask questions on how to choose the right president." Instead of questions, healing testimonies poured in.

The first was a lady in hospital with acute appendicitis, instantly healed. The second had been paralysed, now able to walk. A blind person received her sight. A lump went down instantly on another. A Member of Parliament was healed. The healings were outstanding (all glory be to God!).

Now I knew how to do a radio crusade and have done many over the radio since that time. Then eighteen months later the radio presenter came on radio just after I had spoken and thanked me for speaking on radio every Sunday and said it was good for his radio station that people are healed and that a radio revival was beginning to happen!

Later on in the year the Ebola virus broke out and I was asked to pray against it over the radio. I did. A man from Dura Town then invited Pastor Bobor to come to that town to do a crusade in order to encourage the people (as the Ebola was killing people there). Pastor Bobor did go, but on the Friday, just before the crusade, eighteen people died, so the crusade had to be cancelled. I phoned and asked Pastor Bobor to re-arrange the crusade for radio which he did and a time slot was given to us for 8.00 pm. I gave the Gospel message, the salvation prayer and prayed for the sick. Suddenly the Lord told me to take authority over the Ebola virus over the radio. I remembered John G. Lake took authority over a plague in S. Africa and this encouraged me to obey God. I commanded the Ebola virus to stop right now in Jesus' Name, and that the Ebola die in Dura Town, in Jesus' Name and I brought the radio crusade to an end.

The result was, from that moment on, there was no more Ebola virus in Dura Town and two people were healed from it, as well as one hundred and twenty others healed from various other sicknesses. The people came out on the streets dancing and praising the Lord for delivering their town from the Ebola virus (all glory to God).

We then took authority over another ten towns with the same results and this led to new invitations to speak on radio weekly in Liberia and Nigeria as well. Two months later Bobor was invited back to the eleven towns, not to take authority over Ebola, but instead to encourage the revival that broke out as a result. The churches had grown from 50 to 150 and even 200 in size, as a result of God delivering their towns from Ebola virus. The world news may be slow at declaring good news, but the people saw the truth and power of God with their own eyes and responded accordingly. The

Lord had turned the disaster round for good to bring about the revival.

Let us now take a look at how Jesus conquered the impossible while He was on earth and how He taught us to do the same. We will start with how Jesus came on earth, where the angel Gabriel spoke to Mary about bearing a son and tells her that Elisabeth is also expecting a son in her old age.

Luke 1: 35-37,

> *"And the angel answered and said unto her, The Holy Ghost shall come upon thee, and the power of the Highest shall overshadow thee: therefore also that holy thing which shall be born of thee shall be called the Son of God. And, behold, thy cousin Elisabeth, she hath also conceived a son in her old age: and this is the sixth month with her, who was called barren. For with God nothing shall be impossible."*

(The Greek original of this last sentence actually says that no word from God returns to Him void, just as Isaiah 55.11 says, So shall my word be that goeth forth out of my mouth: it shall not return unto me void, but it shall accomplish that which I please, and it shall prosper in the thing whereto I sent it.)

This shows us that Jesus came to earth in an 'impossible' way through a virgin birth.

Hebrews 10:4,

> *"For [it is] not possible that the blood of bulls and of goats should take away sins."*

Only Jesus was sinless. He was born via a virgin birth, so therefore was not contaminated by the fall of man. He therefore was the only one who could pay the price for our sin.

Acts 2:23,

"Him (Jesus Christ), being delivered by the determinate counsel and foreknowledge of God, ye have taken, and by wicked hands have crucified and slain: Whom God hath raised up, having loosed the pains of death: because it was not possible that he should be holden of it."

Death could not hold Jesus down! Jesus conquered the impossible. Jesus rose from the dead after three days in the tomb. Jesus did the impossible. Jesus conquered sin, sickness and death for each one of us who chooses to receive what He has done for us through our salvation. Not through our own efforts, but by His Grace alone.

Scripture then teaches us how we *can* accomplish the impossible with Jesus.

Mark 9: 23-26,

"Jesus said unto him, If thou canst believe, all things [are] possible to him that believeth. And straightway the father of the child cried out, and said with tears, Lord, I believe; help thou mine unbelief. When Jesus saw that the people came running together, he rebuked the foul spirit, saying unto him, [Thou] dumb and deaf spirit, I charge thee, come out of him, and enter no more into him. And [the spirit] cried, and rent him sore, and came out of him: and he was as one dead; insomuch that many said, he is dead. But Jesus took him by the hand, and lifted him up; and he arose."

Jesus lived the impossible. He had authority and power over distance, over nature, over sickness and over death itself. In these Scriptures Jesus not only shows us what He did but also how He did it.

Jesus then teaches us how to take authority.
Hebrews 11:6,

"But without faith [it is] impossible to please [Him]: for he that cometh to God must believe that He is, and [that] He is a rewarder of them that diligently seek Him."

Without faith the impossible will always stay impossible, but with faith the impossible becomes possible when we *diligently* seek him in prayer.

FAITH COMES WHEN WE BELIEVE THAT JESUS IS ALIVE. FAITH for the impossible is ACTIVATED through PRAYER.

David Hathaway is a man of great faith. He taught me by asking me to become one of his intercessors for Eurovision. He asked me one day to pray for one hundred thousand pounds to come in within a week. "That's impossible Lord," I said, but He replied, *"You give the first thousand pounds and I will cause 99 others to do the same."* I did not want to, that was almost my whole savings, but I obeyed anyway, and within the week the Lord did the rest and the whole amount was raised.

UNBELIEF IS THE GREATEST OBSTACLE TO OVERCOME. If the devil can tempt a person into unbelief, then the impossible will always stay impossible for that person.

Jesus also had problems in dealing with unbelief, even with His own disciples.
Matthew 17:17-20,

"Then Jesus answered and said, O faithless and perverse generation, how long shall I be with you? How long shall I suffer you? Bring him hither to me. And Jesus rebuked the devil; and he departed out of him:

and the child was cured from that very hour. Then came the disciples to Jesus apart, and said, Why could not we cast him out? And Jesus said unto them, Because of your unbelief: for verily I say unto you, If ye have faith as a grain of mustard seed, ye shall say unto this mountain, Remove hence to yonder place; and it shall remove; and nothing shall be impossible unto you."

Faith as small as a mustard seed can move mountains? Well, God created the mountains, did He not? That is how "great" faith is. Faith is stronger than a mountain!! If only we will believe that Jesus is alive: this is the KEY. *IF* Jesus is alive, anything is possible. We are small and insignificant compared to our great big God! We cannot do anything that is impossible, *but* Jesus can, through us. We can break through the impossible with Christ.

While in Zambia, we discovered orphans living alone in the bush or in empty mud huts. We gathered them together for a Gospel Message and to pray for the sick, whom the Lord healed instantly. I could not get back into the car and leave them, there was more to do. "Can anyone teach round here?" I asked. A retired teacher came forward. "If I leave you some money to buy food for these orphans each day, would you be prepared to teach them?" She agreed. I emptied my purse of money and shouted, "Who wants to come to school?" Every hand went up and an orphan school was started, under two mango trees, for eighty seven orphans. Then I got into the car and left.

The only problem was that those orphans increased in number from 87 to 300 within two months. I called an urgent meeting of our Trustees because we did not have the funds to feed all these orphans. I should have asked for permission from the Trustees before I set up this school, but it was extremely difficult when I was in Africa and I could see the need in front of me. I bowed my head in shame at this meeting, not knowing what to do, when the phone rang. It was a lady in Scotland who said, "This morning the Lord told me to give you £5,000 to feed orphans." *The Lord had answered my prayer!* Everything was suddenly sorted out and the same lady later sent enough money to build a school for the orphans.

The Lord supplied the money needed every month through different miraculous ways. Joy Johnson in New Zealand then introduced organic gardening and sank four wells in four villages as the three hundred grew to two thousand orphans!

Today, through the setting up of small businesses, most of our orphans in Africa are now almost self-sufficient – and the *Lord has done it!* All glory goes to Him.

Hebrews 6:18 says,

> *"That by two immutable things, in which [it was] impossible for God to lie, we might have a strong consolation, who have fled for refuge to lay hold upon the hope set before us."*

If it is impossible that God should lie, then what is holding us back, other than our choosing to believe the lies of the devil? The Bible says that the devil is *"the father of lies"* *(John 8:44).*

The Lord showed me that there are three Kingdoms; the Kingdom of Heaven, the Kingdom of darkness and the Kingdom of this world. Through the fall of man the Kingdom of darkness entered into the world, bringing with it sin, sickness and death. The fall of man caused man to live in this world, cut off from the Kingdom of Heaven and so became "spiritually dead." Thus the Kingdom of this world took root. Man became limited to the earthly realm where the impossible stays impossible, because man is born fallen. This is why man cannot understand spiritual things.

1 Corinthians 2:14 says,

"But the natural man receiveth not the things of the Spirit of God: for they are foolishness unto him: neither can he know them, because they are spiritually discerned."

But when man "receives" what Jesus has done for us on the cross he becomes spiritually alive again, born again into the Kingdom of God, becoming a child of God.

This means we are no longer limited to the earthly realm, but can rise up in Christ to break through the impossible with him.

Yet why are most of us not living it? Is it because many of us have received the Lord a little later in life and are so used to living in the limited earthly realm that we receive Christ and just carry on living in the limited realm? Let us rather know who we are in Christ and rise up to our position in Him, where we can live in His victory, just as Jesus did. We can break through the impossible with Christ.

Let us move ahead in faith and believe that the Lord will do it. If we have truly heard from God, then we can also believe that God WILL DO IT.

I gave the Gospel message over the phone to a remote village in Pakistan one day and after praying for the sick, they came forward to share their healing they had just received. A certain lady then complained that for six years she could not see and after prayer she had only been half healed, so could the lady from England please pray for her again over the phone? I prayed for her and suddenly she said she was now completely healed. I thought what wonderful faith she had. If only we all had faith like her, we would also receive our healing so much more easily.

Praying for healing over the phone is also breaking through the impossible with Christ. After all, no doctor can do that! No human being can heal a person over the phone or radio, *but Jesus can and he does all the time. With Jesus we can break through the impossible. The impossible becomes possible because of his great and glorious love for his people.*

For discussion

1. Does this chapter speak to you in any way?

2. How would the Lord like you to respond?

3. What steps should you take?

4. What results are ahead of you?

Orphans gathering

To respond to the Lord for the first time say this prayer below.

> *Dear Lord.*
> *Thank you for dying on the cross for me.*
> *Please forgive me every sin I have ever done.*
> *I choose to follow you in truth and righteousness*
>   *every day of my life.*
> *Thank you for forgiving me.*
> *Please come into my heart and life as my Lord and*
>   *Savior.*
> *Thank you Jesus.*
> *Amen.*

If you have said this prayer you are now forgiven and given everlasting life.

If you are sick, lay your own hand over your sickness or pain and say this prayer.

> *Lord Jesus,*
> *Please lay your hand on my hand,*
> *and I will be healed in Jesus name.*
> *Thank you Jesus.*
> *Amen.*

Now receive your healing in Jesus name, and if you are not instantly healed right now, then pray this same prayer every day until you are healed, and remember God loves you so much and wants you to be healed. God bless you.

From Sin to Righteousness

3

The king or queen rules the country. We are employed by the king as his civil servants. Each worker is given authority by the king to do his/her certain job. The crown or badge is awarded to him/her in that area together with the king's *authority* to carry out that task. It is the same with God's Kingdom.

Prayer is our connection, communication and place for receiving our instructions.

The gifts of the Holy Spirit are the powerful provisions that the King has given to us to accomplish HIS work.

The authority of the Name of Jesus is our authority to get the task done, and our level of authority depends upon our relationship with our King.

The love of God that works through us is comparable to a soldier being prepared to die for his country. It is a sacrificial love for the citizens, a deep desire to rescue them from the clutches of the enemy. In the same way we need to bring the citizens into the saving and healing knowledge of Jesus Christ. The goal is to overcome the enemy (the devil) in every area of life.

This book, therefore, has two purposes. Firstly it is to show that the Lord can equip us to do whatever He calls us to do as a representatives of His Kingdom here on earth. We must know that He has given us the authority of His Name, which is above every name, to do and complete this task.

Secondly it is to show from Scripture the bondage that the enemy has trapped the citizens into, and how to free the citizens from that area of bondage into freedom in Christ, and slowly, inch by inch, person by person, to gain victory in the battleground of this world for the glorious Kingdom of God.

Basically, man gave this earth over to the Enemy, Satan, through the fall of man. Adam and Eve, because they ate of the fruit of the tree of good and evil, gave this perfect earth that had no sin, no sickness and no death, over to our enemy the devil in exchange for the knowledge of good and evil.

This, therefore, allowed three basic curses to enter this world; sin, sickness and death. These three curses have trapped millions upon millions of people in the many different areas of bondage within these three areas. Our great earthly battle, armed with the enablement and the authority given by God from His Heavenly Kingdom, is to discern the different areas of bondage that people are trapped in and then armed with the divine authority of Jesus, to set them free and bring them into the Kingdom of God. We must bring them into new freedom, peace and love: freedom from the curses of sin, sickness and spiritual death, freedom from hate, defeat, and so many more destructive areas, in which man finds himself enslaved.

This book is aimed at leaders as well as those trapped and held prisoner by the Enemy.

Leaders who wish to enrol as one of God's soldiers must learn to walk in the power of the Holy Spirit. To become God's commanders they should know how to walk in the authority of the Name of Jesus and to become God's generals they must know how to walk in the power of God's love.

Those who are imprisoned by the enemy in the different negative destructive forces of evil need to identify the area of bondage, see what the Bible says about that area, and then get set free from that bondage and enter into the peace and joy of victory in God over that area.

Leaders who want to help those struggling in bondage must know that it is impossible to successfully overcome evil forces in their own strength or worldly resources. They have to come into their own personal relationship with God, get victory in Christ themselves and achieve their own *crowns* (meaning victory in that area in Christ) before enrolling as God's ambassadors to set others free.

A leader, therefore, needs to be in total submission to God, to do it only God's way. Never should he do a work on his own strength. It is not man's will, but God's will, not what he thinks, not what he feels, but discerning God's leading about that person or situation. This is done through prayer alone. Once that person has discovered, in prayer and study of God's Word, what God's will is, once he has discovered God's thoughts and His feelings for that person or situation, only then is the leader equipped to help that person to victory in Christ effectively and successfully.

As sin is the major downfall of so many we will start in this area:

"From sin to righteousness"

What is sin? Sin is the deadliest curse of all, more deadly than sickness and more deadly than death itself. Why? Sickness can cause dreadful pain and symptoms in so many different ways, but sickness is restricted to this life only.

Death is the most dreaded thing for so many people, yet that is only the first death. Sin is the worst of the three curses because the wages of sin is death, the first *and* the second death, forever and ever separated from God and Heaven to stay in everlasting darkness and torment.

So why is sin not acceptable to Heaven, some may ask? Well, can I ask those folks this question, "Would Heaven stay as Heaven if sin was allowed in?" The answer to that would be "No," because all sin is caused by hate, hate for God, hate for one another and hate of oneself. If one loved God, one another and oneself then one would automatically keep all Ten Commandments and would not sin.

This is why overcoming sin and walking in righteousness with God is a theme that runs right through the whole Bible. If there were no sin in the world then Jesus would not have needed to die on the cross to make a way out for us, to give us a second chance by receiving His forgiveness, followed by the gift of righteousness and the grace to walk in righteousness.

What makes a person sin? If it was just a rational decision most people would not sin, so what is behind it to influence sin? Feelings. Negative feelings of hate, anger, jealousy, greed, envy, hurt, pride, un forgiveness, mistrust and many other negative feelings. Where do these negative feelings come from? The Kingdom of darkness and who is behind that? The devil himself.

When does a sinner become a sinner? In each area of sin, sinners become enslaved to that sin when the *deceitful* temptation to do that wrong thing appears stronger than their ability to say "No." Hence the sinner has chosen to commit the sin.

The moment they submit to the temptation to do that wrong thing they become weaker than the devil in that area and fall under the devil's power to be tempted more easily in that area. The person becomes weaker and weaker in that area and *"the wages of sin is death."* That is how a person who drinks too much can become an alcoholic, or a person trying out drugs can become a drug addict or a person who tries stealing becomes a thief etc.

All these people *think* they have control, but in actual fact they have lost control of that area and given it over to the Enemy (Satan).

How then can people who have given themselves over to the devil in sin, hope to enter the Kingdom of Heaven? Only one way is open to them and that is *repentance, by this I mean true repentance*, accepting Jesus as Lord of their life. This is to give themselves over to Jesus to save themselves from being under the control of the enemy. Evil entered the world when the first man came under the control of Satan who cunningly persuaded him to eat from the tree of knowledge and good and evil. This is when man gave their authority over to satan, now satan could influence negative feelings from the Kingdom of darkness. It is only though repentance that Jesus rescues us out of the Kingdom of darkness and bring one through to the Kingdom of Heaven where the negative feelings will be replaced with the positive feelings of the fruit of the Spirit which is love Joy peace etc.

Repentance is not just saying sorry. '*Sorry*' in the Concise Oxford Dictionary is described as 'remorse' – sorry for doing it. '*Repentance*', says the same Dictionary, is a radical turnaround. That is exactly right. We need to make a radical turn away from sin to righteousness, to say no to sin and yes to God, no to the devil and yes to God's righteousness, no matter how hard it may appear or what it may cost.

There are three levels of righteousness.

The first level of righteousness is to stop doing wrong through repentance and to follow Jesus in righteousness. To that person who is serious in practicing righteousness, Jesus will give him or her the gift of His righteousness and the grace to achieve it. As the person then abides in His righteousness day by day, the person will become stronger in righteousness to overcome the sin, as he or she is no longer controlled by the devil and his demons. This person forgiven and restored by Jesus will therefore, be able to enter the Kingdom of God, for no sin will be able to hold him or her back. This person shall not enter the Kingdom of God through his or her own effort, but by the grace of Jesus Christ and through the gift of righteousness bestowed upon their lives.

The second level of righteousness is when you have turned from sin, and now you also obey God and do what He tells you in doing good things for others.

The third level of righteousness is through obedience to God's voice, you have now also been filled with His love and obey God out of His love and compassion for others. This is the level of righteousness we should all aim to live.

Matthew's Gospel chapter 16:19, shows that all authority has been given to the believer,

"And I will give unto thee the keys of the kingdom of heaven: and whatsoever thou shalt bind on earth shall be bound in heaven: and whatsoever thou shalt loose on earth shall be loosed in heaven."

Philippians 3:9,

"And be found in Him, not having mine own righteousness, which is of the law but that which is through the faith of Christ, the righteousness which is of God by faith:"

Romans 5:18-19

"Therefore as by the offense of one [judgment came] upon all men to condemnation; even so by the

righteousness of one [the free gift came] upon all men unto justification of life. For as by one man's disobedience many were made sinners, so by the obedience of one shall many be made righteous."

Ezekiel 18:24-28,

"But when the righteous turneth away from his righteousness, and committeth iniquity, [and] doeth according to all the abominations that the wicked [man] doeth, shall he live? All his righteousness that he hath done shall not be mentioned: in his trespass that he hath trespassed, and in his sin that he hath sinned, in them shall he die. Yet ye say, the way of the Lord is not equal. Hear now, O house of Israel; is not my way equal? Are not your ways unequal? When a righteous [man] turneth away from his righteousness, and committeth iniquity, and dieth in them; for his iniquity that he hath done shall he die. Again, when the wicked [man] turneth away from his wickedness that he hath committed, and doeth that which is lawful and right, he shall save his soul alive. Because he considereth, and turneth away from all his transgressions that he hath committed, he shall surely live, he shall not die."

I had a dear friend and discovered she was caught up in a secret sin, a bad sin and I did not know how to address it or even mention it to her, so decided to pray for her instead. A few months later she phoned me and said, *"I have something to tell you that you will not like and don't even know how to tell you."* *"Just tell me,"* I said, and she blurted it out, expecting me to cut our friendship. Instead, I rejoiced that

God had answered the prayer and, after further prayer and repentance, the Lord set her free from that terrible bondage in which she had been caught up.

John 8:3-5,

> *"And the Scribes and Pharisees brought unto him a woman taken in adultery; and when they had set her in the midst, they say unto Him, Master, this woman was taken in adultery, in the very act. Now Moses in the law commanded us, that such should be stoned: but what sayest thou?"*

Look up the above scripture and read on to see that no sin is too great for God to forgive.

When we walk with Jesus, we grow hungry for more of Jesus. Luke 10:38-42,

> *" Now it came to pass, as they went, that he entered into a certain village: and a certain woman named Martha received him into her house. And she had a sister called Mary, which also sat at Jesus' feet, and heard his word. But Martha was cumbered about much serving, and came to him, and said, Lord, dost thou not care that my sister hath left me to serve alone? Bid her therefore that she help me. And Jesus answered and said unto her, Martha, Martha, thou art careful and troubled about many things: But one thing is needful: and Mary hath chosen that good part, which shall not be taken away from her."*

Mary had received her salvation, now she was hungry to hear the teachings of Jesus, to grow in knowing Him as her Lord and Saviour, and Jesus was pleased with this and said that she had chosen the better part, sitting at His feet even though her sister Martha was left with all the serving. The next scripture shows us the more we "know" Jesus, the more we grow in the knowledge of Him.

John 11:32,

> *"Then when Mary was come where Jesus was, and saw him, she fell down at his feet, saying unto him, Lord, if thou hadst been here, my brother had not died."*

Now, Mary knew that if Jesus had come in time He would have healed her brother Lazarus for He was (and still is) the Healer, but then something wonderful happened that caused Mary to pour ointment over the feet of Jesus.

John 12:1-3,

> *"Then Jesus six days before the Passover came to Bethany, where Lazarus was which had been dead, whom he raised from the dead. There they made him a supper; and Martha served: but Lazarus was one of them that sat at the table with him. Then took Mary a pound of ointment of spikenard, very costly, and anointed the feet of Jesus, and wiped his feet with her hair: and the house was filled with the odour of the ointment."*

Why did Mary do such a thing? Was it because Jesus had just raised Lazarus from the dead and was sitting having supper with them? Mary now knew who Jesus *really* was, King of kings and Lord of lords. He was her full salvation unto eternal life.

Salvation is more than just saying the prayer of salvation and going to church. It is a complete radical turnaround from all sin and a turning to God that transforms your whole lifestyle.

It is getting to know Jesus in such a way that the theory of what He did on the Cross becomes the glorious reality in your heart and this brings a freedom and joy that each person wants and needs so much. It also brings a transformation from sadness to joy and from eternal damnation to everlasting life. Our love for God grows stronger and stronger the more we grow in the knowledge of Him.

If anyone reading this book is caught up in any bondage, or in wrongful sexual relationships, you can be totally set free and restored in your relationship with Jesus.

First you need to repent, with a radical turnaround from your sin. You can say this prayer:

> *Lord Jesus,*
>
> *I repent of that sin _____ I make a radical turnaround from it now, never to return to it. I cut off my soul tie now in Jesus' name. I cut off my participation in that sin now in Jesus' name. Please forgive me that sin, Lord. Please come into my heart as my only Lord and Saviour. Please fill the part of my soul, which was in sin and bondage to Satan, with your glorious Holy Spirit.*
>
> *I want to follow you, Jesus, in truth and righteousness every day of my life. Thank you, Jesus, for your forgiveness, grace and love.*
>
> *Amen.*

For discussion

1. What are the three curses that the fall of man caused to come to earth?
2. What is the deadliest curse and why?
3. What does true repentance bring to your life?
4. What is the result of living in righteousness?

From Sickness to Health

4

Historians say that up to 460BC people were sure that all sicknesses were the work of demons. Hippocrates, a Greek physician (c. 460 – c. 370BC), then discovered that sicknesses were of earthly origin. In the 17th century microbes were discovered by Antonie van Leeuwenhoek. In the 1860's Louis Pasteur and others led the way with the "germ theory" as being the root cause of infectious diseases.

I believe that all sicknesses can be "earthly" as well as "spiritual." By this I mean there is a spiritual cause behind the earthly cause of sicknesses. Basically, the devil comes to steal, kill and destroy, but Christ came to give life, and life in abundance (John 10:10). The devil sends sickness to hurt and damage the body and evil spirits to hurt and damage the mind. I will, therefore, treat both in a similar way.

Sickness is the second curse, after sin, to enter this earth because of the fall of man due to his disobedience to God. Sickness attacks the body in many different ways causing pain, discomfort and suffering.

I was always amazed as a child that doctors were so clever, yet there was no cure for a common cold. I was even more amazed when I learnt about germs and viruses. Just when scientists had discovered a way to kill certain diseases, the germs and viruses (so microscopic in size) managed to outwit the doctors by putting up such resistance to medicines that the medicines were no longer effective. This problem has sent the doctors back to square one time and time again, with the invention of even stronger drugs. Now, how can a germ have such great intelligence and power? There has to be another power behind it. I believe the devil is behind every germ, virus and other causes of illness.

There are different ways that sicknesses enter the body.

1. **Germs** If bacteria cause infection or disease, they are commonly called germs. Germs are simple, one celled organisms that exist in most types of environments. Disease-bearing bacteria produce poisons called toxins, treatable with antibiotics. Germs can enter the body through contaminated food or polluted water, a cut, or through insects. Bacterial diseases include sicknesses like cholera, pneumonia, tuberculosis, rheumatic fever and food poisoning.

2. **Viruses** are smaller than bacteria and show no lifelike activity unless they get introduced to a living cell where these viruses can re-produce. Specific viruses are responsible for many diseases including the common cold, influenza, fever, shingles, measles, mumps, chicken pox, polio, rubella and rabies. Antibiotics cannot kill viruses, but vaccinations can stop certain viruses.

3. **Parasites** Parasitic diseases caused by fungal infections or worms.

4. **Nutritional diseases** caused by lack of protein, vitamins or poverty.

5. **Neoplastic disorders** causing tumours or cancer.

6. **Autoimmune diseases** like rheumatoid arthritis that result from a breakdown of the body's ability to recognise its own cells.

7. **Endocrine disease** where the glands fail to produce the right hormones causing diabetes.

8. **Genetic disease** inherited at conception such as downs syndrome.

9. **Degenerative diseases** such as loss of hearing or vision.

10. **Chemical or physical injury** including poisoning, burns, falls or accident.

11. **Iatrogenic disease** (complications) caused by medical treatment sometimes accidental or an after effect of a prolonged drug.

12. **Abuse** of drugs or alcohol.

This very basic look at diseases show us the many ways disease comes into the body via earthly means, that is, gaining entrance through any of the mentioned openings that allow disease to come in.

There has to be an opening for a disease to enter and if the devil is behind every sickness, how does he do it?

Let us look at the list again.

1 & 2) Germs and viruses – through water, food, a cut, an insect bite, through microscopic germs that invade the body so badly. As I have already mentioned, how can a microscopic germ outwit the cleverest of doctors, unless there was an intelligence behind those germs and viruses?

3) Parasitic diseases, caused by fungal infections or worms. They are bigger than germs but resist medicine amazingly quickly causing stronger medicines to be

developed. I believe the intellect behind those worms is also the devil.

5), 6) and 7) where the body fails to work correctly. These disorders can be caused through worry, tension, trauma, sin, unforgiveness. Who is behind these symptoms? I believe it to be the devil again who brought sin, sickness and death into this world.

8) Genetic diseases inherited from our family line (often back to 10 generations) that need to be cut off for any healing to happen.

4), 10) and 11) Lack of vitamins from good food, accidents, falls, burns, after-effects of medicines are certainly from natural causes that can be avoided by walking close to God and looking after ourselves properly.

12) Drug and alcohol abuse is certainly the result of either past hurts, sin, unforgiveness or self-hate.

If the devil is behind all sicknesses or the entry point of those sicknesses to our bodies, then how do we avoid getting sick? We need to look at the Bible and see what the Bible says.
Genesis 3:17,

> *"And unto Adam He (God) said, Because thou hast hearkened unto the voice of thy wife, and hast eaten of the tree, of which I commanded thee, saying, Thou shalt not eat of it: cursed [is] the ground for thy sake; in sorrow shalt thou eat [of] it all the days of thy life."*

Here we read that the ground was cursed. Adam and Eve had given this perfect earth over to the devil in exchange for the knowledge of good and evil. Now the devil has power to inflict sicknesses as well as thorns and thistles through the ground.

Ephesians 6:12,

"For we wrestle not against flesh and blood, but against principalities, against powers, against the rulers of the darkness of this world, against spiritual wickedness in high places."

This verse speaks about the spiritual wickedness in high places, in the air. The devil is also able to send sicknesses through the air. But let us be encouraged by another verse,
Hebrews 4:13 says,

"Neither is there any creature that is not manifest in his sight: but all things [are] naked and opened unto the eyes of him with whom we have to do."

It is encouraging to know that the Lord is omnipresent and can be everywhere at once by the power of the Holy Spirit, but the devil is not omnipresent.
Another Scripture is Ephesians 2:1-6,

"And you [hath he quickened], who were dead in trespasses and sins; wherein in time past ye walked according to the course of this world, according to the prince of the power of the air, the spirit that now worketh in the children of disobedience: Among whom also we all had our conversation in times past in the lusts of our flesh, fulfilling the desires of the flesh and of the mind; and were by nature the children of wrath, even as others. But God, who is rich in mercy, for his great love wherewith he loved us, Even when we were dead in sins, hath quickened us together with Christ, (by grace ye are saved;) And hath raised us up

together, and made us sit together in heavenly places in Christ Jesus."

This also speaks about the prince of the power of the air (the devil), the spirit that now works in the children of disobedience, but God sent us Jesus, who has made provision for us.
Isaiah 53:5,

"But He (Jesus Christ) was wounded for our transgressions, he was bruised for our iniquities: the chastisement of our peace was upon Him; and with His (Jesus') stripes we are healed."

Jesus was whipped 39 times for our sicknesses. It is interesting to know that there are exactly 39 categories of sicknesses and diseases. This means that Jesus has conquered every single sickness, meaning that there is no sickness or disease that Jesus cannot heal.
1 Peter 2:24,

"Who his own self bare our sins in his own body on the tree, that we, being dead to sins, should live unto righteousness: by whose stripes ye were healed."

By whose stripes ye were healed is in the past tense. Jesus has already dealt with every disease and sickness on the cross, therefore all we need to do is receive our healing in Jesus' name.
Psalm 103:3,

"Who forgiveth all thine iniquities; who healeth all thy diseases."

All our iniquities, all our diseases. ALL means ALL! (a 100% completed work)

How has Jesus done this wonderful thing for us? By overcoming the very power of the devil, the power of the air.

Isaiah 45:23,

"I have sworn by myself, the word is gone out of my mouth [in] righteousness, and shall not return, That unto me every knee shall bow, every tongue shall swear."

Romans 14:11,

"For it is written, [As] I live, saith the Lord, every knee shall bow to me, and every tongue shall confess to God."

Romans 14:9,

"For to this end Christ both died, and rose, and revived, that he might be Lord both of the dead and living."

Jesus sealed this victory on the cross and every sickness has a name, every demon has a name, and at the Name of Jesus, each has to bow the knee and obey. By the Name of Jesus they have to bow the knee and GO!

On one occasion in Hexham, Northumberland, I met a man who had been oppressed by a demon for 20 years. He asked me if he could be delivered from it.

I commanded the evil spirit to leave in Jesus' name, but the demon answered me and said, "I shall not leave; this body is my home. I have lived here for 20 years. I will not go back to Hades." I spoke back, very firmly and said, "You have to leave this body right now in Jesus' name. Go now in Jesus' name!" The demon answered back, *"I have to obey*

the name of Jesus, I am going, going, going!" and was gone!
The man was so excited to be free! (All glory to God).

The Lord wants all of us to live free from sin, sickness and
demonic oppression. All of these are influenced by the negative
feelings that are sent on us from the Kingdom of darkness.

3 John 1:2 says,

*"Beloved, I wish above all things that thou mayest
prosper and be in health, even as thy soul prospereth."*

And in the Old Testament, 2 Chronicles 30:20 says,

*"And the Lord hearkened to Hezekiah, and healed
the people."*

How do we get healed?
James 5:16,

*"Confess [your] faults one to another, and pray one
for another, that ye may be healed. The effectual
fervent prayer of a righteous man availeth much."*

All we need to do is ask God in prayer.
Philippians 4:6,

*"Be careful for nothing; but in everything by prayer
and supplication with thanksgiving let your requests
be made known unto God,"*

John 16:23,

*"And in that day ye shall ask me nothing. Verily,
verily, I say unto you, Whatsoever ye shall ask the
Father in my name, he will give [it] you."*

Jesus spent much of His time healing the sick and casting out demons. He healed all who came to Him.
Matthew 4:23,

"And Jesus went about all Galilee, teaching in their synagogues, and preaching the gospel of the kingdom, and healing all manner of sickness and all manner of disease among the people."

Then He sent out the 12, then the 70, to do the same and then told us to do it as well.
Mark 16:15-18,

"And he said unto them, Go ye into all the world, and preach the gospel to every creature. And these signs shall follow them that believe; In my name shall they cast out devils; they shall speak with new tongues; They shall take up serpents; and if they drink any deadly thing, it shall not hurt them; they shall lay hands on the sick, and they shall recover."

James 5:14-15,

"Is any sick among you? Let him call for the elders of the church; and let them pray over him, anointing him with oil in the name of the Lord: And the prayer of faith shall save the sick, and the Lord shall raise him up; and if he have committed sins, they shall be forgiven him."

1 Corinthians 12:27-28

"Now ye are the body of Christ, and members in particular. And God hath set some in the church, first apostles, second prophets, third teachers, after that

miracles, then gifts of healings, helps, governments, diversities of tongues. "

We have discussed different types of sicknesses and diseases, and how they enter the body. We then went to the Bible to find out what Jesus did about it on the cross and that He still heals today through you and me.

SICKNESS IS FROM THE KINGDOM OF DARKNESS

1) A lot of sicknesses and bondages start in the SPIRITUAL realm of darkness brought on by an attack from satan through any opening he can find. These negative thoughts and negative feelings that go with them come from a variety of negatives from your history of hurts, disappointments, failures, abuses, fears, sin and many other things.

2) From the Spiritual it now attacks the SOUL in negative worries, tensions, unforgiveness etc.

3) From the spiritual to the soul to the PHYSICAL BODY in various sicknesses or bondages.

FROM SICKNESS OR BONDAGE TO HEALTH

If you are sick or in bondage, get rid of the cause in every negative thing. Come totally out of the Kingdom of darkness and move yourself through repentance of all negative things into the Kingdom of light, the Heavenly Kingdom. Concentrate on resting in Christ's peace, love, joy, calmness, etc. This causes the sickness to loose its legal right. One can then command the sickness or bondage to leave in JESUS' Name.

BE HEALED IN SPIRIT SOUL AND BODY

1) Search your soul for all negatives and repent from all negative things.

2) Hand everything over to JESUS and do not take anything back.

3) Move your thoughts and soul away from every negative fear to JESUS in the Heavenly realm.

4) Rest and live in Him. In JESUS peace, joy and love is in the Spiritual realm.

5) The peace of Christ is healing, Joy is healing, love is healing.

6) Receive your healing with thanksgiving and walk in your healing.

HEALING IS FROM THE KINGDOM OF HEAVEN

The next question is – How do we pray for the sick?

1. We need to know God in prayer, how to come into His presence and hear Him clearly about the situation we need to pray for.

2. We need to take command over the sickness or disease in Jesus' Name and command the body be healed in Jesus' Name. This is very straightforward and many are healed as a result, but sometimes we are faced with a further challenge if a person does not respond to the healing prayer.

3. If the person does not respond to the healing in any way, we need to ask the Lord for further direction on how to pray. It is amazing how the Lord will answer you. He may take you back to the root of the sickness or disease.

As you mention to the person what the Lord has revealed to you the person may burst into tears. When that happens I know I have heard the Lord correctly and can then lead the person in prayer. Sometimes it will be a prayer of forgiveness towards another person or even for them to forgive themselves. It may be a trauma or hurt from the past. It may be a cutting off from a generational curse or sometimes repentance.

Once the root of the sickness or disease has been dealt with, the healing can happen, sometimes instantly, sometimes more slowly. In Africa they say *"Sometimes God answers like a rocket and sometimes like a tortoise, but He always answers either way."*

A frequently asked question in the West is, "Why does God heal people so easily in Africa or Asia, yet in England or the USA healing seems so much more difficult and many have never seen a healing of God?" Good question.

One answer to that is, desperate people will pray with all their heart, knowing that God will always answer, whereas some people who lack nothing may not pray with all their heart, knowing they have doctors to fall back on.
Revelation 3:15-17,

"I know thy works, that thou art neither cold nor hot: I would thou wert cold or hot. So then because thou art lukewarm, and neither cold nor hot, I will spew thee out of my mouth. Because thou sayest, I am rich, and increased with goods, and have need of nothing; and knowest not that thou art wretched, and miserable, and poor, and blind, and naked:"

In the West people are so rich materially compared to the poverty of Africa or Asia. Yet people in their poverty are often rich spiritually because they have learned to pray with all their hearts, all their soul, all their strength. They will, therefore, receive from God in the same simple hearted way resulting in a beautiful instant healing.

In October 2013 we went to open a new church in a village in India called Shamabadad. There we saw a crippled girl called Shuzeeza. She had been born paralysed from the waist down caused by a twisted spine. Then at 4 years old she also developed polio. She pulled herself across the floor to us with her two arms and responded to Jesus with all her heart. When healing time came after the sermon she was in the line and we prayed for her and asked her "Do you believe Jesus can heal you?" "Yes," she replied. 'Then take my hands and stand up," I said. Her legs were so crippled with turned in feet that we sat her on a chair to pray further for her, when suddenly she shouted, "Look, I can move my knees for the first time in my life, and look, I can wiggle my toes." We told her to exercise her knees and toes every day and then had to leave to visit a new orphanage.

A week later after we returned to England we had an email with the great news that Shuzeeza could now walk. Just as loving God with all our hearts becomes our heartbeat of life, we now see another miracle of a new church being opened in this little girl's village. This has become another heartbeat of life due to God's wonderful healing power (glory to His wonderful Name).

Read Revelation 4:18-22 for more encouragement.

For discussion

1. How many times was Jesus whipped and how many categories of sickness and disease are there?

2. How do we get healed?

3. Why are people healed more easily in Africa or Asia than in Western countries?

4. What did Jesus do to free us from sin, sickness and death and how do we respond?

India crusade

From Death to Life

What is death? What is life? Where is the border line? Are there two deaths?

What can we do about it?

These questions are asked by millions of people and the answers they get are varied, but there is only one correct answer. If death is one of the curses that came into the world due to the fall of man, then we need to take even greater notice.

The 1950 Oxford Concise Dictionary has some very good points to consider:

Death *1) dying, 2) end of life, 3) being killed, 4) ceasing to be, 5) being dead, 6) want of spiritual life.*

Life *1) state of ceaseless change and functional activity peculiar to organised matter, 2) energy, liveliness, vivacity, animation, 3) living things, 4) period from birth to death, 5) fresh start after narrowly escaping death, 6) future eternal everlasting existence after death, 7) active part of existence, business and pleasure of the world, 8) salvation, regenerate condition (also eternal everlasting).*

The New Bible Dictionary says on "death" – *physical decay and ultimate dissolution are inescapable.*

Yet the Bible speaks of "death" as a result of sin. God said to Adam in Genesis 2:17,

> *"But of the tree of the knowledge of good and evil, thou shalt not eat of it: for in the day that thou eatest thereof thou shalt surely die."*

Romans 6:23,

> *"For the wages of sin [is] death; but the gift of God [is] eternal life through Jesus Christ our Lord."*

Yet we see that Adam and Eve did not die "physically" on that day.

Romans 5:12-21,

> *"Wherefore, as by one man sin entered into the world, and death by sin; and so death passed upon all men, for that all have sinned: Nevertheless death reigned from Adam to Moses, even over them that had not sinned after the similitude of Adam's transgression, who is the figure of him that was to come. But not as the offence, so also [is] the free gift. For if through the offence of one many be dead, much more the grace of God, and the gift by grace, [which is] by one man, Jesus Christ, hath abounded unto many. And not as [it was] by one that sinned, [so is] the gift: for the judgment [was] by one to condemnation, but the free gift [is] of many offences unto justification. For if by one man's offence death reigned by one; much more they which receive abundance of grace and of the gift of righteousness shall reign in life by one, Jesus Christ. Therefore as*

by the offence of one [judgment came] upon all men to condemnation; even so by the righteousness of one [the free gift came] upon all men unto justification of life. For as by one man's disobedience many were made sinners, so by the obedience of one shall many be made righteous. Moreover the law entered, that the offence might abound. But where sin abounded, grace did much more abound: That as sin hath reigned unto death, even so might grace reign through righteousness unto eternal life by Jesus Christ our Lord."

Romans 5:6,

"For when we were yet without strength, in due time Christ died for the ungodly."

This compares the death that came through Adam's sin with the life that Jesus Christ brings to mankind. We also see from this passage that life and death includes both physical and spiritual aspects. Man does not just die as a body, but as a "spirit" man and the Bible does not put a sharp line between the two. There is a physical death and a deeper or second death that sin brings on after physical death.

Revelation 2:11,

"He that hath an ear, let him hear what the Spirit saith unto the churches; He that overcometh shall not be hurt of the second death."

Matthew 25:41,

"Then shall he say also unto them on the left hand, Depart from me, ye cursed, into everlasting fire, prepared for the devil and his angels."

Matthew 25:46,

> *"And these shall go away into everlasting punishment:*
> *but the righteous into life eternal."*

John 5:24,

> *"Verily, verily, I say unto you, He that heareth my word,*
> *and believeth on Him that sent me, hath everlasting*
> *life, and shall not come into condemnation; but is*
> *passed from death unto life."*

The Old Testament speaks of Sheol (called Hades in Greek), the dwelling place of all departed spirits (prior to Jesus' resurrection), or the realm of the dead. The New Testament speaks of hell or the lake of fire (called "Gehenna" in Greek). Today, Sheol is the realm of the "lost," a temporary place for those who have died without coming into a saving relationship with Jesus Christ. Their spirits remain there until Jesus' return. They will face the Great White Throne Judgement as described in Revelation 20:11. This is their final judgement prior to the lost being cast into the Lake of Fire, the place of eternal torment and total separation from God.

Revelation 20:11,

> *"And I saw a great white throne, and him that sat*
> *on it, from whose face the earth and the heaven fled*
> *away; and there was found no place for them."*

Prior to Jesus' resurrection from the dead, the Scriptures tell us that the departed righteous spirits were in a different area of Sheol called "Paradise" or Abraham's bosom (read Luke 16). Once Jesus had made a way for our full atonement (brought us back into a right relationship with God) these righteous spirits ascended to heaven. This happened when Jesus died, was buried and rose again.

Ephesians 4:8-10,

> *"Wherefore he saith, When he ascended up on high, he led captivity captive, and gave gifts unto men."*

(Now that he ascended, what is it but that he also descended first into the lower parts of the earth? He that descended is the same also that ascended up far above all heavens, that he might fill all things)."

Mathew 27:52,

> *"And the graves were opened; and many bodies of the saints which slept arose."*

This speaks of man to die once as in his physical death, but the time for decision is over and then would come the judgment. The second death is his spiritual death. This would come at the time of the White Throne Judgment. This means we must be prepared and ready for death in advance. If you want to go to Hell you do nothing. If you want to go to Heaven, accept Jesus as Lord, for it is His work on the cross alone that makes the way for each one of us. Death is not the end of a person, for God breathed into him the breath of life causing a living being. Revelation 1:18 says,

> *"I [am] he that liveth, and was dead; and, behold, I am alive for evermore, Amen; and have the keys of hell and of death."*

We only have this life to decide between "Heaven" or "Hell." The Bible is the only book that discusses Heaven and Hell.

Other religions try and show a way to heaven through good works, but the Bible teaches us how to get there, as good works are not enough, for all have sinned.

There are three phases to life.

1. Present life in our mortal bodies – the shortest phase. Yet the most vital phase. It is here in "this earthly realm" that we make the decision for Heaven or Hell, righteousness or sin, eternal life or eternal death.

2. Physical death, where it is too late to make a decision, is our intermediate phase. For the nonbeliever, a temporary stage but nevertheless a place of no escape from spiritual death.

3. The raising of believers to a resurrected glorified body, where we enter eternal life. For the believer this is "spiritual life", eternity with the Lord in Heaven. The empty grave proved the resurrection of the body of Jesus who conquered our enemies of sin, sickness and death on the cross. Accepting what Jesus did for us gives us the very same victory over sin, sickness and over death itself.

Revelation 14:13,

> *"And I heard a voice from heaven saying unto me, Write, Blessed [are] the dead which die in the Lord from henceforth: Yea, saith the Spirit, that they may rest from their labours; and their works do follow them."*

Philippians 1:20-24,

> *"According to my earnest expectation and [my] hope, that in nothing I shall be ashamed, but [that] with all*

boldness, as always, [so] now also Christ shall be magnified in my body, whether [it be] by life, or by death. For to me to live [is] Christ, and to die [is] gain. But if I live in the flesh, this [is] the fruit of my labour: yet what I shall choose I wot not. For I am in a strait betwixt two, having a desire to depart, and to be with Christ; which is far better: Nevertheless to abide in the flesh [is] more needful for you."

2 Corinthians 5:1,

"For we know that if our earthly house of [this] tabernacle were dissolved, we have a building of God, an house not made with hands, eternal in the heavens."

The Lord then showed me a vision. I was out in space, looking down at the world revolving on itself as it went round the sun. This is what causes day and night, weeks, months and years. Behind the world is what looked like a trail of a comet. At the very back of the trail I saw the word Genesis. At the centre of the trail I saw the cross and just in front of the world I saw the word Revelation. The Lord then said to me "That is the realm of time. The world revolving on itself giving day and night as it revolves around the sun gives you the years.

And the time span from Genesis to Revelation is all contained in your Bible, with the history of all mankind. And for you my children, your personal time span, is from the moment you are conceived till the moment you die physically. That is your earthly life on earth. After that you enter the eternal realm."

These words were of great encouragement to me.

These Scriptures end with the faithful promises of God:

John 11:25-26,

"Jesus said unto her, I am the resurrection, and the life: he that believeth in Me, though he were dead, yet shall he live: And whosoever liveth and believeth in me shall never die. Believest thou this?"

2 Corinthians 5:8,

"We are confident, [I say], and willing rather to be absent from the body, and to be present with The Lord."

This is why we should share the Good News of what Jesus has done for us. In order to go from death to life spiritually do the following: thank God that He has made a way for all of us to choose "life." When a believer closes his eyes today, he has assurance that he will be with The Lord. Physical death for the believer only leads to "spiritual life." Thank you Jesus!

1. Accept Jesus as your Lord and Saviour.

2. Pray daily and get to know Him. Give Him a specific time each day.

3. Read your Bible, privately and with others in your church or fellowship.

4. Live the Christian life in righteousness.

If you have not made this very important decision yet and would like to receive Jesus as Lord, say this prayer with me:

Lord Jesus, thank you for dying on the cross for me. Please forgive me for every sin I have ever done. I choose now to follow you in truth and righteousness every day of my life. Thank you for forgiving me. Please come into my heart and life as my Lord and Saviour. Thank you Jesus. AMEN!

For discussion

1. What brought physical death into the world?

2. What can we do to escape the second or deeper spiritual death?

3. Name four things we can do after accepting what Jesus has done for us on the cross.

4. Have you said the prayer above? If not, think of what you can lose and what you can gain by receiving Jesus as Lord.

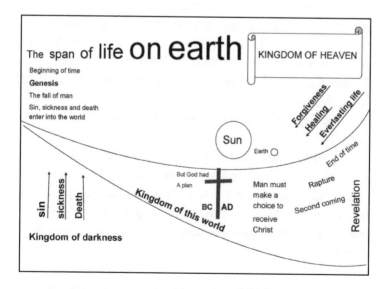

From Bondage to Freedom

Many Christians everywhere are not walking in the victory that Jesus has made available for them. They feel unworthy to serve God, inadequate and fearful. All sorts of things bind them to such a level that it is hard for them to break free.

Some people are still harbouring unforgiveness against another person or against themselves or carry a past hurt. Others are bound by a past trauma caused by an accident or abuse, physically or emotionally. Yet others just believe a lie that they heard against themselves at some time in their lives. All of these negative feelings are sent to steal kill and destroy, from the Kingdom of darkness. Read John 10 verse 10.

All these issues are very real, even though they are just spiritual things that are holding them back. These spiritual forces can attack the mind in such a way that the person is bound down, unable to move forward or get free from it. There is some good news for these people from the Word of God.

Colossians 2:13-15,

"And you, being dead in your sins and the uncircumcision of your flesh, hath he quickened

together with him, having forgiven you all trespasses;
Blotting out the handwriting of ordinances that was
against us, which was contrary to us, and took it
out of the way, nailing it to his cross; [And] having
spoiled principalities and powers, he made a shew of
them openly, triumphing over them in it."

This verse says three very important things to us.
Colossians 2:13 says that we are forgiven because
Jesus has already paid the price for all our sins on the
cross. Colossians 2:14 says that His death on the cross
also wiped out all the requirements of the Law of the
Old Testament.

Romans 10:4 says,

"For Christ is the end of the law for righteousness to
everyone who believes."

and Romans 6:14 says,

"For sin shall not have dominion over you: for ye
are not under the law, but under grace."

When you confess your sins and accept Jesus as Lord and
Saviour you are forgiven and made righteous by faith in
Jesus, therefore you are no longer "under" the governance of
that Law. Yet how many Christians still walk in the yoke of
bondage to the Law or to the old spiritual problems that have
held them down, possibly for many years?

Colossians 2:15 has dealt with this so well,

"Having disarmed principalities and powers, He
made a public spectacle of them, triumphing over
them in it."

This means that Jesus disarmed his enemies, stripping them of all their armour and weapons. Jesus triumphed over them and subjected them to an open total defeat. Jesus has totally defeated all principalities and powers who were in rebellion against God and man. All the devil has got left is to bluff and deceive us into staying in his terrible bondage, when we can become totally free through Jesus.

It all comes down to whom we believe, Satan or God. We no longer need to live in fear, hoping somehow to hold Satan off, if we know that Jesus has already disarmed the devil.

Jesus gave man dominion over all the earth in Genesis 1:26. It is man who gave his dominion over to Satan through eating the fruit of the knowledge of good and evil, but God did something about it. Jesus came not only to pay the price for this sin on the cross and forgive us but also set us free and give us back the dominion of the earth.

Genesis 1:26,

> *"And God said, Let us make man in our image, after our likeness: and let them have dominion over the fish of the sea, and over the fowl of the air, and over the cattle, and over all the earth, and over every creeping thing that creepeth upon the earth."*

Revelation 1:5,

> *"And from Jesus Christ, [who is] the faithful witness, [and] the first begotten of the dead, and the prince of the kings of the earth. Unto him that loved us, and washed us from our sins in his own blood."*

Jesus is the firstborn from the dead. He has become the "Prince of kings of the earth." *He* is our Prince and Ruler, not Satan anymore, not since Jesus died and rose from the dead.

Psalm 89:26-27,

*"He shall cry unto me, Thou [art] my father, my God,
and the rock of my salvation. Also I will make him
[my] firstborn, higher than the kings of the earth."*

Psalm 2:4-7,

*"He that sitteth in the heavens shall laugh: the Lord
shall have them in derision. Then shall he speak unto
them in his wrath, and vex them in his sore displeasure.
Yet have I set my king upon my holy hill of Zion. I will
declare the decree: the Lord hath said unto me, Thou
[art] my Son; this day have I begotten thee."*

Jesus is the head of the new race and we are part of it, if we
have accepted Jesus as Lord.
1 Peter 1:3,

*"Blessed [be] the God and Father of our Lord Jesus
Christ, which according to his abundant mercy
hath begotten us again unto a lively hope by the
resurrection of Jesus Christ from the dead."*

Not only did God 'beget' Jesus, but He begat (and continues
to do so) those who come to Him, into a "living hope
through the resurrection of Jesus Christ from the dead". Jesus
identified Himself with us, forgiving our sins and setting us
free from all bondages so that we may be identified with
Him in His righteousness, victory and triumph.
Ephesians 2:5-6,

*Even when we were dead in sins, hath quickened
us together with Christ, (by grace ye are saved;)*

*And hath raised [us] up together, and made [us] sit
together in heavenly [places] in Christ Jesus."*

We are identified with Christ in the sight of God, in that
God made us alive with Christ and raised us up together
with Christ and made us sit in heavenly places in Christ. As
Jesus has identified Himself this much with us, we can in
turn identify ourselves with Him also in His death, burial,
resurrection and ascension.

What does this mean to us? Hosea 6:1-2,

*"Come, and let us return unto the Lord: for he hath
torn, and he will heal us; he hath smitten, and he will
bind us up. After two days will he revive us: in the third
day he will raise us up, and we shall live in his sight."*

This is a call to repentance, opening the way for our healing
and restoration. Hosea speaks to us that we are raised up
with Christ. God not only raised Jesus from the dead, but all
of us who have received Jesus, plus His whole body, that is,
"the Church" who have received Him. Jesus has done it all
for us from His side. He has only one thing for us to do and
that is for us to rise up in Him, in prayer, and take authority
on His behalf against our enemy the devil, against those evil
spirits of unworthiness, fears, rejections, hindrances, abuses,
unforgiveness, addictions etc and cast them out in Jesus'
name! Even as Adam was in charge of creation, so we, with
Christ's authority, have dominion.

Luke 9:1,

*"Then he called his twelve disciples together, and
gave them power and authority over all devils, and
to cure diseases. And he sent them to preach the
kingdom of God, and to heal the sick."*

Then to the seventy, He said, in Luke 10:17-20,

"And the seventy returned again with joy, saying, Lord, even the devils are subject unto us through thy name. And he said unto them, I beheld Satan as lightning fall from heaven. Behold, I give unto you power to tread on serpents and scorpions, and over all the power of the enemy: and nothing shall by any means hurt you. Notwithstanding in this rejoice not, that the spirits are subject unto you; but rather rejoice, because your names are written in heaven."

2 Corinthians 10:3-5,

"For though we walk in the flesh, we do not war after the flesh: (For the weapons of our warfare [are] not carnal, but mighty through God to the pulling down of strongholds;) Casting down imaginations, and every high thing that exalteth itself against the knowledge of God, and bringing into captivity every thought to the obedience of Christ."

God has provided us with the spiritual weapons to fight this spiritual war. These spiritual attacks on our lives are sent to stop us from becoming victorious Christians.

John 10:10,

"The thief cometh not, but for to steal, and to kill, and to destroy: I am come that they might have life, and that they might have [it] more abundantly."

The devil *does* come to steal, kill and destroy and will sometimes attack us as young children to try and destroy our lives. Many people do not realise that they are not the only ones who have been through a hardship or trauma, in fact about 50% of mankind have experienced in many different ways abuse, trauma, unfairness, hurt or loss in some way or other. This has often caused the person to live in the negative results caused by these unfortunate things that have happened to us. The negative results will be in relation to the cause. Abuse will cause fear of man, fear of rejection, poor self-esteem, etc. Trauma may cause insecurity. Hurt may cause anger, etc.

To get set free we need to come to the Lord and bring Him with you back to the time when the trauma or problem happened and give it to Him so that He can remove it from you and bring you into healing.

I was abused by a trusted babysitter at the age of three. I thought I must have been naughty somehow to be hurt so badly and this caused me to feel shame from the wounding and then, because my parents were dealing with the babysitter, I fell asleep before they could pick me up, causing rejection. It also caused a terrible fear of man and this affected my life for many years, as I was afraid to tell anyone in case they did not understand me.

One day I did tell someone who kept taking me back to the trauma which I did not enjoy. Then they asked me, "What does Jesus say about it?" So I asked Jesus, who said it was not my fault. Then He said "I am very pleased with you." This made me cry with relief as I realised that He thought of me in a positive way. This helped me a lot but did not entirely set me free.

A year later I mentioned this to a trusted friend who again took me back to the same trauma. This time I saw a vision of Jesus picking up a three year old child out of a cot and holding this child close to His breast. I did not think further of it until I went to sleep that night.

I was that child Jesus had picked up out of the cot and I was crying bitterly into His loving arms and I cried on and on. Then, suddenly thinking I had cried far too long in His arms I looked up into His glorious face. He said to me, "I have all the time in the world for you, my precious child" and He cupped his beautiful soft hands around my head and pressed me very gently back into His lovely warm chest, where I cried with joy at His beautiful words to me and the more I cried the lighter and freer I felt.

I awoke the next morning with my face wet from the tears feeling freer than I ever hoped to be. I sat up in excitement, realising I had spent the whole night with Jesus and this has had a big impact on my life. It has caused me to see life differently and caused me to become more confident and far less fearful.

Getting fully free of the negative things that the devil has managed to bring into your life can take years, yet every prayer gets another layer of suffering out of your life. Just like an onion, you have to remove one layer at a time and with each layer yet another negative thing is removed from your life, bringing you into freedom as the Lord's child.

Ephesians 1:5-6,

"Having predestinated us unto the adoption of children by Jesus Christ to himself, according to the good pleasure of his will, To the praise of the glory of his grace, wherein he hath made us accepted in the beloved."

And 2 Corinthians 10:4 says,

"For though we walk in the flesh, we do not war after the flesh: (For the weapons of our warfare [are] not carnal, but mighty through God to the pulling down of strongholds;) Casting down imaginations, and every

high thing that exalteth itself against the knowledge
of God, and bringing into captivity every thought to
the obedience of Christ."

In Christ we have the victory, total victory over every
depressive spirit, in Jesus' Name.
   Hebrews 12:2

   "Looking unto Jesus the author and finisher of [our]
   faith; who for the joy that was set before him endured
   the cross, despising the shame, and is set down at the
   right hand of the throne of God."

Because of what Jesus has done for us on the cross, everything
we need to be set free from has been conquered.
   We can break through the impossible through the mighty
Name of Jesus and if you would like to be set free right now,
please say this prayer below.

   Lord Jesus, I come to you now. I lift up this spiritual
   problem to you right now and I command this
   spiritual problem_____ leave me right now
   in Jesus' Name. Get out now in Jesus' Name.
   I thank you Lord that you love me; I receive your
   deliverance now in Jesus Name and believe you want
   me to live completely free from this thing from this
   time on. Thank you Jesus. Amen.

And if you need to forgive someone or forgive yourself,
choose to forgive in this prayer.

   Lord Jesus I choose to forgive _____
   in Jesus' Name. I forgive them now in Jesus' Name.
   Thank you Jesus. Amen.

Now read Ephesians chapter 2, for this will re-affirm your faith of what Jesus has done on the cross for you.

> *Lord, I lift this person up to you that he or she may realise who he or she is in you, Your beloved child. Thank you, Lord, that You want to raise this person up to a new level of walking in You and that You have given this person authority and power over the Enemy. This person will now walk in this new victory in You as a result. Thank you, Jesus. Amen.*

For discussion

1. Name some of the bondages that hold people down.

2. What did Jesus do to set us free from bondages?

3. What must you do to be set free from a bondage?

4. What does it mean to you to be free?

Telephone evangelism

From Rejection to Acceptance

When a hurt, abuse, trauma, sickness, curse, sin, shame or rejection takes its toll on a person, it is very hard for that person to find acceptance in Christ.

They will feel unworthy. Often they think it was their fault that the unfortunate bondage came upon them and that they deserved the punishment upon their lives. Others even think that it is the Lord who is punishing them and accept their sickness or bondage as from God rather than the devil.

Whether it is sin, sickness, loss, bondage, abuse or hurt, there is some good news for you.

Isaiah 53:3,

"He is despised and rejected of men; a man of sorrows, and acquainted with grief: and we hid as it were [our] faces from him; he was despised, and we esteemed him not."

This means we can give Jesus our rejection for He has taken our rejection upon Himself on the cross and given us His acceptance in exchange.

By His grace Jesus also gives us His supernatural blessings of forgiveness, healing, deliverance, peace, acceptance and love.

Jesus wants to rescue us from all negative feelings sent on us from the Kingdom of darkness and bring us into His Kingdom of Heaven, for the Kingdom of Heaven is at hand.

Ask the Lord for His revelation of what He has done for you personally on the cross.

Acts 10:34-35,

"Then Peter opened [his] mouth, and said, Of a truth I perceive that God is no respecter of persons: But in every nation he that feareth him, and worketh righteousness, is accepted with Him."

Romans 12:2,

"And be not conformed to this world: but be ye transformed by the renewing of your mind, that ye may prove what [is] that good, and acceptable, and perfect, will of God."

We are then fully acceptable to God.

Ephesians 1:3-6,

"Blessed [be] the God and Father of our Lord Jesus Christ, who hath blessed us with all spiritual blessings in heavenly [places] in Christ: According as he hath chosen us in him before the foundation of the world, that we should be holy and without blame before him in love: Having predestinated us unto the adoption of children by Jesus Christ to himself, according to the good pleasure of his will, To the praise of the glory of his grace, wherein he hath made us accepted in the beloved."

The problem is not that God does not accept us, but often it is people themselves who will not accept themselves, usually because they have not forgiven themselves or the person who has hurt them, or they are struggling with shame and rejection from an abuse or trauma from the past.

This was the result I had in my life from the time I was abused by the babysitter. I shut myself off, even from my own parents and could not tell anyone what had happened to me. My mother wanted to give me her beautiful gold crown necklace as a gift, but I turned it down feeling unworthy to wear it, but then something wonderful happened to me. Jesus set me free through that wonderful dream of crying into His glorious arms that whole night and this freed me.

This freed me up enough to phone my brother, as both our parents had now passed on by this time. I asked him, what had happened to Mom's gold crown and he said it was in his safe, after all he couldn't wear it. I told him what had happened to me and he said, "Would you like to have the crown?" I said "Yes, please." He replied, "I would love to give you the crown as a birthday present" and did. I now wear this beautiful crown because I feel accepted by the Lord and, because *He* has accepted me, I have accepted myself as well.

On a personal level, even though it took years, the Lord took my negative crown of thorns and gave me the crown of victory. My gold crown necklace reminds me of this victory every time I wear it.

The Lord wants to do the same for you.

Jesus did a complete work for us on the cross and all we need to do is identify ourselves with what He has done for us. We need to know that He endured rejection that we may become free of it. He has also paid the price for our sin, our shame, our failure, our bondage. The Lord may not deal with you in the same way as He dealt with me, but

He will deal with you in a unique way that He will reveal to you.

Choose to identify yourself with what He has done for you. Choose to forgive yourself and accept yourself, just as Jesus has forgiven you and is waiting to accept you now as His own beloved child. You may say this prayer below.

Lord, I come to you now. Thank you for forgiving me.

I now choose to forgive myself and those who have hurt or abused me. (Name out loud those whom you need to forgive in Jesus' Name.)

I choose to accept myself now as you have accepted me, in Jesus' Name.

Thank you, Jesus, Amen.

For discussion

1. The Lord has exchanged every negative thing in our lives with His positive blessings on the cross. How do we then identify ourselves with what He has done for us?

2. Name negative things that can hold you back.

3. Name some positive blessings that the Lord wants to give to you.

4. What changes would you like to receive in your own life? Would you like to ask Jesus for them?

CHAPTER 8

From Poverty to Abundance

It was hot and dusty, we had undertaken a long journey to get there. David's car had broken down once and in another place a lorry nearly backed over us both in our car which really made us pray overtime!! 'S-u-e' exclaimed David afterwards, seeing the expression on my horrified face, and then laughed. We both laughed with relief. Only one headlight had been damaged as the lorry had stopped just in time.

This was my second trip to Ghana in 2004 and my first trip to the rain forest region. The people were very poor and their mud huts did not look very inviting for two weary travellers. We also struggled to find the right track to the place of meeting where our hosts were waiting.

Eventually we found the place of meeting. A very thin lady showed me to an old brick building where to my surprise, I actually had a bed to sleep in. The old lady gave me a bucket of water to bath with. We also had some food to eat and, after the meal, went to bed.

First thing the next morning they informed me that I needed to pay a courtesy visit to the King of the rain forest.

I had never stood in front of a King before, so I went rather unprepared with David and the kraal leader.

We entered the courtyard of the King and David introduced me to the him. There he sat upon his throne holding a sceptre in his right hand and on either side of him sat six elders on chairs. The courtyard was also full of people who were also sitting on chairs. They were all in their traditional dress with only one shoulder covered.

David led the way for me to shake hands with the six elders on our right. I followed him. David then bowed before the King and shook hands with him. I then curtseyed before the King and then shook his hand as well. We then went to the six elders on the left side to shake their hands. I was then led to a seat in the front, in the centre of the gathering of people facing the King. I was then told to sit.

The King stood up and greeted me. I stood up and also greeted him. The King then said to me, "You have a word from the Lord God for me, speak now." I was totally unprepared and fumbled for my Bible and just opened it anywhere.

My eyes fell on Deuteronomy: 30:15-16,

"See, I have set before thee this day life and good, and death and evil;

In that I command thee this day to love the Lord thy God, to walk in his ways, and to keep his commandments and his statutes and his judgments, that thou mayest live and multiply:"

The Lord then told me to turn back a page and read it to the King.

Deuteronomy 28:15-24,

"But it shall come to pass, if thou wilt not hearken unto the voice of the Lord thy God, to observe to

do all his commandments and his statutes which I command thee this day; that all these curses shall come upon thee, and overtake thee:

Cursed [shalt] thou [be] in the city, and cursed [shalt] thou [be] in the field.

Cursed [shall be] thy basket and thy store.

Cursed [shall be] the fruit of thy body, and the fruit of thy land, the increase of thy kine, and the flocks of thy sheep.

Cursed [shalt] thou [be] when thou comest in, and cursed [shalt] thou [be] when thou goest out.

The Lord shall send upon thee cursing, vexation, and rebuke, in all that thou settest thine hand unto for to do, until thou be destroyed, and until thou perish quickly; because of the wickedness of thy doings, whereby thou hast forsaken me.

The Lord shall make the pestilence cleave unto thee, until he have consumed thee from off the land, whither thou goest to possess it.

The Lord shall smite thee with a consumption, and with a fever, and with an inflammation, and with an extreme burning, and with the sword, and with blasting, and with mildew; and they shall pursue thee until thou perish.

And thy heaven that [is] over thy head shall be brass, and the earth that is under thee [shall be] iron.

The Lord shall make the rain of thy land powder and dust: from heaven shall it come down upon thee, until thou be destroyed."

I was shaking with fear of what the King might do to me as well as in the anointing of what the Lord was doing at the same time. Then the Lord told me to read:

Deuteronomy: 28:1-10,

"And it shall come to pass, if thou shalt hearken diligently unto the voice of the Lord thy God, to observe [and] to do all his commandments which I command thee this day, that the Lord thy God will set thee on high above all nations of the earth:

And all these blessings shall come on thee, and overtake thee, if thou shalt hearken unto the voice of the Lord thy God.

Blessed [shalt] thou [be] in the city, and blessed [shalt] thou [be] in the field.

Blessed [shall be] the fruit of thy body, and the fruit of thy ground, and the fruit of thy cattle, the increase of thy kine, and the flocks of thy sheep.

Blessed [shall be] thy basket and thy store.

Blessed [shalt] thou [be] when thou comest in, and blessed [shalt] thou [be] when thou goest out.

The Lord shall cause thine enemies that rise up against thee to be smitten before thy face: they shall come out against thee one way, and flee before thee seven ways.

The Lord shall command the blessing upon thee in thy storehouses, and in all that thou settest thine hand unto; and he shall bless thee in the land which the Lord thy God giveth thee.

The Lord shall establish thee an holy people unto himself, as he hath sworn unto thee, if thou shalt keep the commandments of the Lord thy God, and walk in his ways.

And all people of the earth shall see that thou art called by the name of the Lord; and they shall be afraid of thee.

And the Lord shall make thee plenteous in goods,

in the fruit of thy body, and in the fruit of thy cattle, and in the fruit of thy ground, in the land which the Lord sware unto thy fathers to give thee.

The Lord shall open unto thee his good treasure, the heaven to give the rain unto thy land in his season, and to bless all the work of thine hand: and thou shalt lend unto many nations, and thou shalt not borrow."

I then shared the gospel message of how Jesus won the victory over the curses of sin and death on the cross.

"We are delivered from these curses when we believe in Him and accept Him as our Lord and Saviour" I ended with.

The King stood up again and said, "I receive these words and we will do it." He then summoned his gong beater to come forward. A thin elderly man appeared holding a piece of wood and a gonger on the end of a wooden handle.

"I command you," said the King "go out to every village and every kraal and summon every person to come to the village crusade tomorrow at the main gathering field." The gong beater left immediately to do the job. I then presented the king with a Bible and left.

The next day over three thousand people arrived for the crusade including the King's elders who all sat in the front row in their traditional clothing. I gave the gospel message and most of them stood and repeated the sinner's prayer after me.

We then prayed for the sick and many were healed. One lady who had a broken collar bone was instantly healed. The next day she went to the doctor for another X-ray to find the collar bone perfectly healed and in line. She brought the X-rays of the injury, before and after, to show us the perfection of the Lord's healing.

The King did as he had promised and built churches, one for each village. He then asked us to send some money for the cost of the iron sheets to complete the roofing. This we sent him. The result was that the blessing of God came on the newly converted villages with excellent crops, large fruit and vegetables and twin goats being born several times. So the entire area has gone from poverty to abundance. This year 2014, 10 years later, David is again visiting the blessed rainforest region to encourage the people.

The Bible is just as powerful now as it was those many years ago. Deuteronomy spoke of poverty caused by humiliation, oppression, shortage, barrenness, family breakdown, failure, physical or mental illness, God's rejection and God's disfavour.

The blessings of abundance are that blessings shall overtake you, fertility, prosperity, victory, health, and God's favour when we obey the Lord.

Deuteronomy 28.13,

"And the Lord shall make thee the head, and not the tail; and thou shalt be above only, and thou shalt not be beneath; if that thou hearken unto the commandments of the Lord thy God, which I command thee this day, to observe and to do [them]:"

This speaks of God's children being the head and not the tail that gets dragged around. We must respond to Jesus and He will make you the head.

Isaiah 53.3-12,

"He is despised and rejected of men; a man of sorrows, and acquainted with grief: and we hid as it were [our] faces from Him; He was despised, and we esteemed Him not.

Surely He hath borne our griefs, and carried our sorrows: yet we did esteem Him stricken, smitten of God, and afflicted.

But He [was] wounded for our transgressions, [He was] bruised for our iniquities: the chastisement of our peace [was] upon Him; and with His stripes we are healed.

All we like sheep have gone astray; we have turned every one to his own way; and the Lord hath laid on Him the iniquity of us all.

He was oppressed, and He was afflicted, yet He opened not His mouth: He is brought as a lamb to the slaughter, and as a sheep before her shearers is dumb, so He openeth not His mouth. He was taken from prison and from judgment: and who shall declare His generation? for He was cut off out of the land of the living: for the transgression of my people was He stricken.

And He made His grave with the wicked, and with the rich in His death; because He had done no violence, neither [was any] deceit in His mouth. f Yet it pleased the Lord to bruise Him; He hath put [Him] to grief: when thou shalt make His soul an offering for sin, He shall see [his] seed, He shall prolong [His] days, and the pleasure of the Lord shall prosper in His hand.

He shall see of the travail of His soul, [and] shall be satisfied: by His knowledge shall my righteous servant justify many; for He shall bear their iniquities. Therefore will I divide Him [a portion] with the great, and He shall divide the spoil with the strong; because He hath poured out His soul unto death: and He was numbered with the transgressors; and He bare the sin of many, and made intercession for the transgressors."

And in the New Testament we read in John 12:4-8 of Mary pouring ointment over the feet of Jesus. Judas, who carried the money bag, asked why the money was not used for the poor.

Jesus never carried money, but never lacked. Jesus always met the need. He turned water into wine at the wedding feast. He multiplied food for the 4,000 and the 5,000 and he still meets our needs for you and me today. I have seen Him multiply breakfast for us at a youth camp and I have seen Him supply for our orphans month after month. He has always met our need.

Yet He came to die on the cross in our place, where He suffered our poverty, our hunger and thirst, our nakedness and even our rejection.

Mathew 27:46,

"And about the ninth hour Jesus cried with a loud voice, saying, Eli, Eli, lama sabachthani? that is to say, My God, my God, why hast thou forsaken me?"

But JESUS loved the Father and knew the Father loved Him so his last words were "And when JESUS cried out with a loud voice, He said Father, INTO THY HANDS I COMMEND MY SPIRIT and having said thus, He gave up the Ghost. (Luke 23:46)

We too need to believe God and not the situation or feelings we are facing.

Jesus bore our rejection upon the cross. He did all this to free us from every curse the devil has placed on us.

Gal 3:13,

"Christ hath redeemed us from the curse of the law, being made a curse for us: for it is written, Cursed [is] every one that hangeth on a tree:"

And Jesus also redeemed us from the curse of the Law and gave us His grace.

2 Corinthians 8:9,

> *"For ye know the grace of our Lord Jesus Christ, that, though he was rich, yet for your sakes he became poor, that ye through his poverty might be rich."*

2 Corinthians 9:8,

> *"And God [is] able to make all grace abound toward you; that ye, always having all sufficiency in all [things], may abound to every good work:"*

Jesus has done a complete work for us on the cross. He has delivered us from every curse, every demon, every sickness and from all forms of poverty and brought us into his blessing instead.

All we have to do is come to Jesus and choose His forgiveness, His deliverance, His healing and receive His blessings into our lives.

We will also notice that God's prosperity does not speak about money, but about blessings that go far beyond money alone. They are blessings that money cannot buy. When we realise this, then we are able to give to the Lord's work in whatever way that is needed and the Lord will also look after us.

I have also noticed in my own life that you cannot out give God, for the more you give or do for others, the more the Lord gives and does for you.

My earthly father taught me that everything you do good in life you get back double as good, and every bad thing you do in life you get back double as bad. I make sure I only do what is good.

If you have suffered curses or poverty in your life, you may choose life and prosperity now. Turn from any curses or sin in Jesus' Name. As you do this seriously and turn to Jesus, to follow Him with all your heart, you will be amazed how He will turn your life around from this day on.

For discussion

1. Name some of the curses in Deuteronomy.

2. Name some of the blessings in Deuteronomy.

3. Name some of the curses Jesus set us free from on the cross.

4. How do we receive freedom from curses in our own life?

Presenting a Bible to the Rain Forest King

Breaking Through the Impossible in Prayer

We held an all-night prayer vigil to pray in the New Year 2014. We connected by phone to pray with 8,200 teachers, evangelists, pastors and students across 18 countries of Africa and Asia, who were praying and fasting with us in their various countries. We also had a one hour broadcast with a radio in Freetown, Sierra Leone.

After many phone calls we settled down to hot mince pies, coffee and some serious prayer and waiting on God. As we waited on God He spoke to all of us individually on the same thing, how to break through in the spiritual realm. Once we had this victory in prayer in the spiritual realm, the answer came in the physical realm. The Lord then reminded us of times when we had done this in the past, even without realising it and the results of instant healings that had happened in the physical. He also showed me how we had had to pray to turn back storms on various occasions in prayer and then saw God's answer in stopping the storm, so that our crusades could commence. He also showed us times when we had not prayed and therefore did *not* see change. It was up to us.

Matthew 16.19,

"And I will give unto thee the keys of the kingdom of heaven: and whatsoever thou shalt bind on earth shall be bound in heaven: and whatsoever thou shalt loose on earth shall be loosed in heaven."

The Lord showed us so clearly that in 2014 we were to pray seriously and break through each situation in prayer first and then the victory would be ours, in our lives and ministries. We would see God's answers every time, because prayer activates the answers, beginning in the spirit realm and *then* the answer to prayer would become active in the physical realm. We should always remember that prayer comes before service.

Prayer seems to be answered to the degree we ask. We can either live in a hazy distance from God in prayer, where we will only hear Him in a limited way, or we can draw deep into God's presence, face to face, Spirit to spirit. If we do this, we will *know* that He hears us and we will be able to hear Him clearly. As we then obey Him and do what He tells us, the Lord Himself will confirm what He has told us, 'with signs and wonders following'. We will find ourselves breaking through the impossible with Him.

I believe God has allowed evil to stay in the world to teach us how to pray, how to take authority through spiritual warfare and prepare us for the future, when one day we will rule with Christ for all eternity.

Revelation 3.21,

"To him that overcometh will I grant to sit with me on my throne, even as I also overcame, and am sat down with my Father on his throne."

Matthew 16.18-19,

> *"And I say also unto thee, That thou art Peter, and upon this rock I will build my church; and the gates of hell shall not prevail against it. And I will give unto thee the keys of the kingdom of heaven: and whatsoever thou shalt bind on earth shall be bound in heaven: and whatsoever thou shalt loose on earth shall be loosed in heaven."*

Luke 10.19,

> *"Behold, I give unto you power to tread on serpents and scorpions, and over all the power of the enemy: and nothing shall by any means hurt you."*

John 20.21-23,

> *"Then said Jesus to them again, Peace [be] unto you: as [my] Father hath sent me, even so send I you. And when he had said this, he breathed on [them], and saith unto them, Receive ye the Holy Ghost: Whose soever sins ye remit, they are remitted unto them; [and] whose soever [sins] ye retain, they are retained."*

John 14.13,

> *"And whatsoever ye shall ask in my name, that will I do, that the Father may be glorified in the Son. If ye shall ask any thing in my name, I will do [it.]."*

John 15.7,

*"If ye abide in me, and my words abide in you,
ye shall ask what ye will, and it shall be done
unto you."*

These are amazing verses! God has intended us to pray so
He that can answer. God wants us to have victory over all
evil and God will give us the victory when we pray because
this is His will. In prayer God will train us how to get victory
in spiritual warfare and overcome evil. He will teach us how
to live in prayer and then He can use us to change the lives
of others.

John Wesley said, "God will do nothing but in answer
to prayer." S. D. Gordon said, "The greatest thing anyone
can do for God is to pray. You can do more than pray after
you have prayed, but you cannot do more than pray until
after you have prayed. Prayer is striking the winning blow –
service is gathering up the results."

The more praying there is in the world, the better the
world will be, for answered prayer is far stronger than the
forces of evil.

Prayer should therefore be the most important part of
every day. Alexander Maclaren said, "much prayer for the
cause by those at the home base means power released on the
field, and that weakness at the home base means weakness in
the field." I find this so true.

In 2012 Joy Johnson in New Zealand and I were
trying to get the four orphanages in Zambia self-sufficient,
as it was costing over £2,000 a month to feed the
3,000 orphans there.

The Lord has answered Joy's prayers by leading her to
sink wells for water and establish organic gardens and this
proved an effective way of reducing our costs.

I then prayed about how to supply the staple diet of maize or similar feed, which would need a lot more land and the Lord said to me, "Tell David the orphanage farmer to ask the Chief to give the orphanage 125 acres of land." I immediately phoned David and told him what God had told me. David went to the Chief and the Chief said, "Yes" and gave the orphanage 125 acres of land.

David then ploughed up the land and planted the maize towards the end of 2012 and it grew well. In January 2013 I got a worried phone call from David. "Millions of caterpillars have eaten up half the maize crop!" he exclaimed. "What should I do?" "Who gave us the land?" I asked. "The Lord," he replied, "through the Chief." "Then," I answered, "go down to the land and command the caterpillars 'die in Jesus' name!'." David obeyed and did the job. Next day he went to inspect the land and found that every caterpillar was dead. He re-ploughed the land and replanted more seeds. We had an excellent harvest and the orphans had food for the next six months, which meant that only a little money was needed for food. To the Lord be the glory!

Towards the end of 2013 David asked for more money to buy seeds, because the hybrid seeds could not be replanted as they only do one crop. This sent us back to prayer and Joy discovered a place up north in Zambia, whose Chief would not allow his people to grow hybrid seed, only traditional seed that does not need fertiliser and can be replanted each year.

Joy sent David up-country to buy the seeds. Instead of feeding this valuable re-plantable maize to the orphans, we swapped it with all the local farmers for planting, in exchange for hybrid maize for eating. This enabled the whole community to return to planting the old type of traditional, re-plantable seed, so that a percentage of the maize is kept back to plant for the following year and the balance can be eaten. This would bring the whole community back to the way God designed it in the first place by the 2015 harvest, and save our ministry the seed money each year. God is so good and so, so practical!

From Heaven's point of view all spiritual victories are won in prayer. This will always cause the victories in the practical realm.

Yet so many people ask, *"How do I even approach God, let alone get into His presence?"*

I would now like to spend some time on this important question.

When Wilfrid and I returned from New Zealand in 2011 the people in our house decided to surprise us by re-carpeting the prayer house and removed the altar to do so.

I am afraid I was not too happy about this and went straight into prayer, as they had thrown away the prayer basket and the letters in it, not knowing they were all from sick people needing miracles from God.

"Lord," I prayed, "they threw away the prayer basket with all the names of the sick people in it!"

"Don't worry," the Lord replied, *"I have every name of every person on my heart. They only threw the papers away."*

"And, Lord," I went on, "what about the altar they took down?"

"Don't worry about that either, build Me a prayer tabernacle after the pattern I gave Moses in the wilderness."

"How?" I asked.

"I will show you how", the Lord answered.

The Lord did show us how and within three months it was completed. I thought that it would be a good teaching tool on prayer and it is, but it is also much more as well.

I would like to share with you about what the Lord has taught me from this Tabernacle about approaching God in prayer as well as overcoming the many hindrances in prayer.

The Tabernacle was given to Moses to build on their way from Egypt to the promised land, and is likened to a journey into prayer, as well as our journey as believers towards our promised land Heaven. Everything in the Tabernacle looks to Jesus our Saviour, who frees us from the bondage of Satan and then through baptism we become reborn as one of God's children, similar to the crossing of the Red Sea, freeing the Jewish Nation from slavery to the Egyptians. The Jews could have reached their promised land far sooner, but through disobedience it took forty years. Our journey into prayer is also connected to obedience. Disobedience will hinder us just as greatly in our walk with God.

The Tabernacle has three sections. The first part deals with the flesh and sin. The second part deals with the soul, the will, the mind and the emotions. The third part deals with the Spirit that brings us into the presence of God. The devil will try and prevent us from praying in the first two areas, but cannot touch you in the third part, the Holy of Holies. He knows that once you come into this place of worship he cannot touch you.

The "Outer Court" deals with the flesh and sin. This was the place they sacrificed sheep and goats for the forgiveness of sin. This all looks to Jesus as the one and only perfect sacrifice. Here we also wash our feet, likened to the reading of the Bible that cleanses us from the inside. God does not look at outside appearances but rather what we look like from the inside, walking in truth and righteousness.

The "Outer Court," therefore, is a picture of the first level of prayer of confessing any sin, and receiving forgiveness.

We then try and approach God, but this is where we have the most distractions, the phone rings, someone knocks on the door or calls you, etc. This is probably why most of us need to pray at 5 am to avoid so many distractions.

As we press on in prayer we enter the next area, the Holy Place, which has three items of furniture, the table of show bread, the candlestick and the table of incense. We will start with the table of show bread. The bread being baked symbolises the different aspects of the will. Are we finely ground to do God's will, or do we want to do what we want? Are we moulded to joyful, yielded obedience or do we obey with difficulty? Do we give up when tested, or do we press though to victory? Do we pray as we should? Are we disciplined? All these things correspond to bread being baked. It is here where we have to fight with the "will." The "will" wants to sleep or give up etc, but it is not about what we want but what God wants, so we press on in prayer.

Next, we come to the lampstand that deals with the mind and intellect. Do we accept all Scripture, or only the scriptures we like? Here we may battle with our mind, intellect or reason, but the important thing is not what we think but what Christ thinks. We need Him to renew our minds so that we come into agreement with all Scripture, all of God's counsel, and to think more like Jesus.

Then we come to the "table of incense" which deals with our emotions. We may not yet have felt the presence of Jesus and may want to give up, but it's not about what *we* feel but what Jesus feels. When we press on regardless in prayer, it is only then that we break through from the soul to the spirit, right into the Holy of Holies, spirit to Spirit, face to face with God.

In the Holy of Holies there are three levels of prayer, WORSHIP, FELLOWSHIP and REVELATION.

Worship brings us right into God's presence and we know it is wonderful in His presence. We may be standing, sitting, kneeling or face down and it is here that we know He hears us.

As we spend time in His presence, our busy, rushed minds quieten down to a place where we can hear the Lord's still small voice. For this reason we must never rush through prayer or we will miss the most important part, hearing His voice.

Some people will listen to 'soaking music' or their favourite Christian music, to help them relax into prayer and enjoy the Lord's presence, as they enter into deeper prayer.

This will draw us into fellowship with God, where we can discuss the various issues we are facing and hear God's advice on how to handle each one. The Lord will open up the scriptures to you and teach you, give you revelation and speak into your life.

When it comes to praying for others, do not give the Lord a 'shopping list' of requests. It is better to bring Him one request at a time and ask Him how He wants to answer it and how He wants you to pray.

If He wants to use you in the answer, He will give you His revelation of what He wants you to do about these things. Pray through one request at a time and pray until you know the Lord has answered your prayer, when His peace comes upon you.

You then enter the area of revelation, where He speaks to you, with His revelation of what He wants you to do about the matters you have prayed about, or a divine appointment He may have for you.

When we come out of prayer in this way, we come out still feeling His divine *kavod* presence in our hearts, which may stay in us for the rest of the day. In addition we know exactly what He wants us to do and how to do it. If we walk

IN CHRIST in this way, our lives and work for Him are guaranteed to be successful.

A command from the Lord will often entail a sacrifice or inconvenience. We need to break though this to the victory the other side. The devil will give you many excuses why you should not do it, but when we make that choice to obey God regardless, even in difficulties, the results will always be a blessing. I can share many testimonies of this being so true. I have had to go into countries like Pakistan, Burma and Nigeria, through fear, wanting to get on the next bus home rather than getting on the plane, yet, when I go regardless, the Lord has protected me and blessed the trips there so much. He has done what I could never do; He has healed the sick, set people free and brought many to salvation.

After all, who are we? In God I mean. Scripture describes us as kings and priests, a holy nation.

1 Peter 2:9-10,

"But you are a chosen generation, a royal priesthood, an holy nation, a peculiar people; that ye should shew forth the praises of Him who called you out of darkness into His marvellous light. Which in time past you were not a people, but are now the people of God: which had not obtained mercy, but now have obtained mercy."

What does this say to us?

Firstly we have to be Holy, knowing the difference between right and wrong and seriously living for God in full truth and righteousness, separated from the world, yes living *for* God and His people, loving and obeying Him.

Secondly, we need to live as His New Covenant people, His kingly church, living in His light, in His Holy Spirit, above sin, shielded from the fiery darts coming from the powers of darkness, abiding in living contact with our Lord and King through prayer and obedience.

I am so glad that our living God knows what is going on in the world and has His solution to all the problems, injustices and wars. He is coming back very soon now. We belong to Him in holiness to live as His kings; to love His people, helping them to see the truth, helping them to be free from the attacks of the enemy and find their destiny in God.

Thirdly, we are God's Priests who are able to stand in the gap in prayer for people, to intercede and fast for them, until we hear God speak and show us how to minister to them. This is the greatest service we can give our Lord, to really seek Him, hear Him and obey Him.

We are living in difficult times these days when humanism has taken over in all areas of life. The dictionaries describe humanism as the denial of any power or moral value superior to that of humanity. The Oxford dictionary describes 'humanism' as devotion to human interests, a system concerned with human (not divine) interests, or with the human race (not the individual); religion of humanity; literature, culture, especially that of the humanists; also students of human nature or human affairs, especially in the (Renaissance) 14th-16th centuries, of Roman and Greek literature.

I find this quite scary. Even in our universities, we are now taught in a different way to conform with this new outlook, causing people to criticise and judge the very Word of God that orders our daily lives.

An Anglican priest told me recently that "People either believe the Word of God and come under it, or don't believe the Word of God and come above it."

It is so true, and such thinking as to 'come above' the Word is very dangerous, because it leads to pride and rebellion. Satan, who didn't fear God, tried to do the same thing to God and fell, thrown out of Heaven for all eternity.

On the other hand if one bows down and 'comes under' the authority of the Word of God, one finds life, and life in abundance.

John 3:16,

"For God so loved the world, that He gave His only begotten Son, that whosoever believeth in Him should not perish, but have everlasting life."

2 Timothy 3:16,

"all scripture is given by inspiration of God, and is profitable for doctrine, for re proof, for correction, for instruction in righteousness: That the man of God may be perfect, thoroughly furnished unto all good works."

This is the great safety of believing and coming under the Word of God.

◊ Let us make our relationship with God through prayer and the reading of His Word into a dynamic life-changing victory of knowing Him, knowing His will for our lives and living our lives in His truth and righteousness in full victory IN HIM.

◊ When praying, the key to hearing God speak to you is your yielded obedience. Not what I want but what the Lord wants, not what I think but what the Lord thinks, not what I feel but what the Lord feels. When we yield to Him in this way we are putting the Lord first.

◊   It is then that He speaks to us, and, as we simply obey Him and His instructions, we will find ourselves breaking through the impossible with Him. WHY? It is because the Lord is doing it. He simply uses us to do what He tells us and He does what we cannot do.

◊   Our battles and victories are all accomplished in prayer. When we get God's answer in prayer then it is also activated in the physical realm.

◊   Let us learn to trust Him completely, knowing that He is in control and He shall surely DO IT!

It is the Lord's desire that every believer is able to break through the impossible with Christ.
     Luke 1:37,

"For with God nothing shall be impossible!"

AMEN

For discussion

1. How can we effect change in our own lives?

2. What areas do I need to break through in my own life as I enter into serious prayer?

3. Why is it important not to approach God hastily, but to wait on Him?

4. If we hear God, we must obey God. Why?

Breaking Through to the Beauty of Yielded Obedience

There are different levels of yielding and different levels of obedience.

The more yielded and obedient you are to God, the more He can achieve through your life.

The Tabernacle the Lord gave to Moses in the wilderness shows our progression into worship, holiness and wholeness through the three areas. The outer court deals with sin and the flesh, the inner court with your soul and the Holy of Holies with your spirit.

It was only recently that the Lord showed me that the Tabernacle does not just stop at worship but involves your whole lifestyle. The Lord needed to take me through this Tabernacle yet again at a new and very exciting level and took me into the Word to explain everything to me as we went through it.

He started of course in the outer court, showing me that this is the area a new believer turns to Christ and has to deal with his sin and flesh.

Turning from sin must be a radical turnaround from all sin in sincere repentance, from the old sinful life to new life in Christ. Jesus died on the cross for us and we need to die to the flesh and all sin to live for Him. Not like the world.

Romans 10.3,

"For they being ignorant of God's righteousness and going about to establish their own righteousness, have not SUBMITTED themselves unto the righteousness of God."

Don't we see that around us in our world right now? Political correctness is replacing part of righteousness and I wonder how long it will take to turn into political control.

James 4.7-8,

"SUBMIT yourselves therefore to God, resist the devil and he will flee from you. Draw nigh to God and He will draw nigh to you."

For this is what Jesus has done for you.

Philippians 2.8,

"Though He were a Son, yet learned obedience by the things He suffered and being made perfect, He became the author of eternal salvation unto all that OBEY Him."

We see here that submission and obedience to God starts right here in the outer court, a decision that begins the first steps of your journey with God and the reward for this is in Hebrews.

Hebrews 12.11,

"Now no chastening for the present seemeth to be joyous but grievous, nevertheless afterwards it yieldeth the peaceable fruit of righteousness unto them which are exercised there by."

The next level is the INNER COURT THE HOLY PLACE which deals with the soul and the three different areas of our lives that need to be submitted to God.

The three items of furniture are not only levels of prayer, but of YOUR LIFE AND SERVICE also.

The table of show bread deals with your will, the candlestick with your mind and intellect and the table of incense with your emotions, a lot of yielding and submission, but not without a promise.

Exodus 19.5,

"Now therefore, if ye will OBEY my voice indeed, and keep my covenant, then ye shall be a peculiar treasure unto me above all people; for all the earth is mine. And ye shall be unto me a Kingdom of priests, and an holy nation."

These are words given to the Jewish nation, but Gentiles are the wild olive branches who have been grafted into the vine, therefore Gentiles are also included in this promise.

As you start with the table of showbread and yield your will to God in the same way as described in chapter 9 of this book, you will find different levels of submission. Flour has to be ground very fine. Your "will" needs to become smooth and fine like flour. Then it has to be moulded. Are you conformed to the will of God? Then the bread has to be baked. Are you ready for the Lords testing? Then the bread needs to be in two rows of six in good order. Are you disciplined? The bread is now covered with frankincense showing submission in worship. Then the table of incense is surrounded by two crowns that teach us to watch and pray. There is part level, full level or UNCONDITIONAL surrender, where you can say, "Not my will, but your will be done". I highly recommend you read *"Entering the presence of God"* by Derek Prince who goes into full detail regarding the Tabernacle.

Acts 5.29,

> *"Then Peter and the other apostles answered and said, "We ought to obey God rather than men."*

Yes, there is often a conflict of the will; your will and the will of others around you. But when you sacrifice your own will and what men want you to do, a blessing always awaits you if you do the will of God instead.

Leviticus 26.13,

> *"If ye walk in my statutes, and keep my commandments and do them, then I will give you rain in due season, and the land shall yield her increase and the trees of the field their fruit,"*

The CANDLESTICK is next, representing your mind and intellect. By yielding up your mind to the Lord, He will bring it in line with the Bible until you think like Jesus.

Isaiah 56.8-9,

> *"For my thoughts are not your thoughts, neither are your ways my ways, saith The Lord. For as the heavens are higher than the earth, so are my ways higher than your ways, and my thoughts than your thoughts."*

It is therefore not what we think, but what The Lord thinks. When you yield to thinking as He thinks, then you will also be able to hear His thoughts and to speak out His thoughts rather than your own.

When we learn to do this, even against the grain of what we think, a further promise awaits us.

Exodus 23.22,

*"But if thou shalt indeed obey His voice and do
all that I speak, then I will be an enemy unto your
enemies and an adversary unto thine adversaries."*

I am reminded of the time I had to correct a church in Kenya.
This church was not moving forward at all and half of them
were sick. They sat silent in their pews quite unresponsive.
I asked the Lord what to do and He said, "Take them to
the market." I did not want to. I did not think they would
like to go. I did not think it a good idea but I chose to obey
God anyway.

When I said, "We are now going to the market," they
looked at me in horror. "Pick up your chairs, we are going
now, and bring the guitar as well." We all crowded outside
reluctantly and I said, "Let us sing some praise songs on the
way." Well, if I ever heard half-hearted singing come from
Africans, it was then.

We walked to the market singing and found a suitable place
to preach from. We sang two songs and I got up to preach the
Gospel message, in such a way that all who were hearing it
would stop and listen to the whole message. The crowd got
larger and larger, then I called anyone who needed healing to
come up and the crowd watched excitedly as Jesus instantly
healed each person who came up. I then simply said, "Who
wants to receive this Jesus as Lord and Saviour?" Hands went
up everywhere. We led them through the sinner's prayer, told
them where our church was and we walked back.

That night the church was crowded to capacity and the
original congregation, having seen the power of God in their
midst, were totally changed and most were also healed.
This church then realised that church was there to teach and
encourage them how to witness to others and they have had

two outreaches a month since that time and have planted new churches as a result.

Another time in Texas I had to minister to a soup kitchen for 30 minutes a day before their meal. I could not get through to them, so I prayed about it and the Lord said, "Identify yourself with them." Not easy to obey as they were the worst assortment of alcoholics, drug addicts, sinners and destitute people that I had ever seen. I had to go against what I wanted to do or thought about it and obey God regardless of how I felt.

Next day I stood up and said, "You think I am just another speaker from England who has never suffered anything. I want to tell you now that I am just like you. We have all suffered the results of sin, sickness, abuse and unfortunate circumstances, but it does not matter what got us into these situations, but rather how we handle them. We can allow ourselves to be pulled down by them further and further, or we can stand up and do something positive about the problems we are in. Would you like to know how?"

They all put their hands up and I shared what Jesus had done for us on the cross, and then asked those who would like to become free to come forward. One by one most of them came forward and in tears received Jesus and were set free by Jesus. The Holy Spirit came down upon all of us as we hugged each other with tears of Joy. Jesus had done it again.

I did not want to go to India in January 2015. It was the week after the announcement on TV by the prime minister of India that Hindus wanting to persecute Christians would not be punished. As we prayed about it The Lord did not say he would not allow activists to come, but He did say He would protect us.

Elizabeth and I went. We were to speak daily with ten other local speakers to a seven day conference to over ten thousand daily. On the third day twenty armed activists turned up minutes after we left the platform and we hid in a room praying for their salvation. Next day they came again and waited most the day to catch us, but we remained in the room until they had gone. Once they were gone we were called to deliver our message. The third day the same thing happened, but on the fourth only ten came. They had been so impacted, so convicted by the word of God on the previous three days, that they wanted more of God and two of them were baptised that very day.

God wants us to put our prayers into action, not just "say" prayers. He told a good friend of mine that He was "*weary of pretty prayers*." Anyone can pray a beautiful sounding prayer, but unless he is also prepared to action it, it will not mean much. When we action our prayers then the Lord will reveal His ways and His miracles, and will amaze us through what He will do.

The final area of the soul is the TABLE OF INCENSE, the emotions. Emotions with some people can be up and down, but when we give our emotions to the Lord we are giving Him much more, we are giving Him our very heart and soul as well.

Psalm 34.22,

"The Lord redeemeth the soul of His servants: and none of them that trust Him shall be desolate."

Giving the Lord our emotions means getting our heart to come into line with our spirit man. Your heart is the container for your soul, spirit and Holy Spirit.

As you give your heart and soul and emotions to the Lord, He will give you his rest and you will find yourself starting to walk in His Spirit. The Lord will then give you His grace to walk in the Spirit. The Lord is the supplier of His Peace, His Joy, and His rest. The more you yield your life to surrendered obedience, the greater will be your lifestyle change.

I have trained many horses throughout my life. You can only train a horse once he has yielded to you in trust and allows you to train him. The more the horse yields himself to you, the greater will be his training until the horse not only yields his body to you in obedience but his mind as well. When this happens you have the makings of a champion who is obedient to the lightest of signals through your weight aids, hands and leg aids until you move as one, horse and rider dancing to music in dressage, or clearing the high fences demanded in show jumping. In the same way we need to trust God like a horse trusts his rider and become so sensitive to His small still voice and to the lightest touch of His guiding hand.

The next level is in the Spirit as you enter THE HOLY OF HOLIES right into the spiritual realm, spirit to Spirit, heart to heart, face to face with God. In this area striving ceases as you enter into love, worship and rest. Enjoyment of service now replaces sacrifice, in that sacrifice does not appear to be sacrifice as you willingly yield your will, mind and emotions to achieve what the Lord has placed on your heart.

As you pour out your love for God, something wonderful happens, He also pours out His love into your heart and a heart to heart connection takes place. As you spend time in this glorious place in Him, His Holy Spirit fills every cell in your being until you can barely contain it. It can feel as if you are going to burst if you do not share His wonderful salvation with others or pray for the sick and watch the Lord heal them. When you pray for others, it appears that every cell responds, as the life of God through the Holy Spirit flows through your hands to the afflicted place of the person you are praying for bringing healing.

His will has become your will and a oneness of service has resulted. This brings a bonding of love of working with

Him. You connect with God on this new level into His work, His ways and His victories.

You now walk in fellowship with the Lord, where you can discuss your life or ministry with Him, asking for His directions, His answers and His way of doing things. As you do this, you will hear His voice and He will give you His revelation of what He is doing and your part in it.

As you then obey the Lord and do exactly what He has told you to do, He will confirm what He has told you to do with His signs and wonders following.

Not only that but further promises will follow you.

1 Peter 1.22,

> *"Seeing ye have purified your souls in obeying the truth through the spirit unto unfeigned love of the brethren, see that ye love one another with a pure heart fervently, being born again not of corruptible seed, but incorruptible, by the word of God, which liveth and abideth forever."*

And,

Revelation 22.14,

> *"Blessed are they that do His commandments, that they may have the right to the tree of life, and may enter in through the gates into the city."*

◊ The world is preparing the way for the antichrist,

◊ But God is preparing the way for the second coming of Christ.

◊ The devil is preparing the world to receive the Mark of the Beast,

◊ But Jesus is preparing His people to receive the gift of Faith.

◊   The cross to the world is offensive

◊   But to the Christian it is the Joy of Salvation.

◊   The second coming of Christ will be terror to the unrighteous

◊   But to the believer, it is the transfer into eternal life with Christ.

We come back to the first paragraphs of this book where one day we will stand before God and the angels will enter in and present you with your crown.

If we have lived this life in our own strength, one might be tempted to place the crown on one's own head, but if you have lived your live for Christ, you can do no other than lay your crown down at the feet of Jesus, representing your life given for Him.

Yielding and obedience to our Lord is not easy! Yielding is a daily process for each one of us, just as repentance is. There will be seasons in our life where we sense that our emotions are getting the better of us, but if we stay close to our Father in heaven (who knows exactly what we are going through and sees the thoughts and intents of our heart), we will grow and mature in Him. Sometimes, the more we go through, the more we see the faithfulness of God and it becomes easier to yield to Him, because we know that the Lord won't let us down.

How do we yield? It is talking to the Lord about every area of your life. We know when we are falling away, so to speak. If we examine ourselves, our lifestyle, we will know where we need to make changes. Let us begin by talking to Him about whatever it is that seems to be coming between us and Him; then giving Him permission to "take it" because it may have become a burden to us or even a blockage. We read in Psalm 23 that "He restoreth our soul". There may come a time in our life especially after a loss of a loved one or similar situation, when The Lord may need to "restore the soul". Now this is the time to give the Lord permission to do this. Have you ever thought that if the Lord has been given permission to heal your soul, then He may want you to "walk in the Spirit" now! Yielding up our emotions can be a very liberating experience, knowing that God is now in control! This yielding of things to the Lord can cover every area of our lives, from our own desires and plans or our ministry. It can cover our pains and hurts, as well as overcoming temptations of any kind. "Just hand them over" to the Lord and make a decision not to take them back again. Keep on yielding them up to Him. Ask the Lord to give you His grace to help you do this.

The pure joy (of the Lord) that lies ahead for that person is glorious, such that no sacrifice, no difficulty or hurt endured in this life can ever compare. It appears to me that the Lord yielded all of His being to God, even to enduring the cross on our behalf. Resurrection from the dead was waiting for Him, and after that ascending to Heaven itself where He now sits in glory at the right hand of His Father. In the same way, all the suffering we may have to endure on earth, whether it be sickness or the most difficult of situations, when we give it all to God and yield our lives to Him, a glorious future awaits us. All becomes so small compared to our eternal life in Heaven with Jesus. Let us all yield to Him with unconditional surrender and obedience and allow the King of kings and Lord of lords to work His glorious works through our lives given for Him.

Let us give our lives now in unconditional surrender to Him, who has done so much for us. When we do this you will be amazed at what the Lord may do in and through our lives and when we stand before Him one day we will be able to do no other than lay the crown He has given us at the feet of Jesus and enter eternal life with Him.

For discussion

1. What has this chapter meant to you?

2. What changes would you like to make?

3. How would you like to go about bringing the changes into action?

4. What do you think the changes will result in your life for the Lord?

Books by Suzanne Pillans

Testimonial Book
Dare to Search for Truth
On Prayer
Dare to Enter His Presence
Dare to do only the Father's Will
On Discipleship
Dare to Step Out in Faith
Dare to Walk in Power, Authority and Love

The Standlake Equestrian Centre and Ranch
Downs Road, Standlake, Oxfordshire, OX29 7UH
Contact Phone: 01865 300 099
Email: suzannesministries@gmail.com
www.suzannesministries.co.uk
www.standlakeranch.co.uk

We hope you enjoyed reading this New Wine
book.For details of other New Wine books and
a wide range of titles from other Word and
Spirit publishers visit our website:
www.newwinebookshop.com
or email us at newwine@roperpenberthy.co.uk